The Prepper's Long Term Survival Handbook

Step-By-Step Guide for Off-Grid Shelter, Self Sufficient Food, and More To Survive Anywhere, During ANY Disaster in as Little as 30 Days

Small Footprint Press

Table of Contents

INTRODUCTION 1

   WHO IS SMALL FOOTPRINT PRESS? 4

CHAPTER 1 THE BASICS OF SURVIVAL................... 6

   WHY DOES WILDERNESS SURVIVAL MATTER?....... 6

   SURVIVAL GEAR CHECKLIST 14

   RESCUE ITEMS... 20

   MISCELLANEOUS SURVIVAL ITEMS........................... 20

   SURVIVAL MENTALITY 21

**CHAPTER 2 WATER: WHERE TO FIND IT AND
HOW TO USE IT** 28

   FINDING WATER.. 29

   PURIFYING WATER... 36

**CHAPTER 3 DON'T STARVE: FINDING FOOD IN
THE WILD**...40

   THE IMPORTANCE OF FOOD... 40

   WHERE TO FIND FOOD.. 41

   PYRAMID OF WILDERNESS SURVIVAL FOOD........ 45

   TIERS OF WILDERNESS FOOD...................................... 46

CHAPTER 4 STAYING WARM....................................54

   WHY STAYING WARM IS IMPORTANT 54

   STRATEGIES FOR DRESSING PROPERLY AND
   SHELTER BUILDING... 57

   BUILDING A FIRE 60

CHAPTER 5 FIRST AID **65**

NECESSARY FIRST AID SKILLS 65

COMMON HOUSEHOLD ITEMS FOR FIRST AID 67

SKILLS EVERYONE SHOULD LEARN.......................... 68

CHAPTER 6 DEFENDING YOURSELF IN THE WILDERNESS **76**

WHY IS LEARNING SELF-DEFENCE NECESSARY? 76

SITUATIONS YOU MAY ENCOUNTER 76

SELF-DEFENSE TECHNIQUES 78

CHAPTER 7 BUILDING A SHELTER **88**

WHY IS SHELTER IMPORTANT? 88

A WIDE ARRAY OF SHELTERS 89

HAVING A BACKUP SHELTER 102

CONCLUSION **104**

REFERENCES **105**

Introduction

Our society is becoming increasingly unstable—our world functions in more unsustainable ways with each passing day. With the planet's growing population, an affinity for a faster-paced life, advancements in technology, and a preference for an increasingly self-centered lifestyle for many individuals, our environmental resources are being depleted faster than we can imagine. Our current situation shows that in the future, we may have to seek alternative ways to live. Let's imagine that the unthinkable happens, and say a global market crash, a world-altering natural disaster, famine, or large-scale war occurs. At that moment, we'll realize that the need to be prepared for such things is absolutely crucial. But it's no use waiting for these kinds of disasters to take place. It's time to act now. But you may ask, where do I even start? The answer is simple: educate yourself on what to prepare for, the ways you can prep, and how. After learning more about it, you can then take the practical steps to build a framework to create your plan of action. The prepping lifestyle isn't just about stocking piles of food and water. It starts with changing your mindset that foresees events before they take place and taking the proper action to mitigate the effects of these events. There is a common notion among non-preppers that preppers are paranoid kinds of people. But nothing could be further from the truth! Preppers are simply individuals that have developed a mentality to plan for the future, take the initiative in taking care of themselves and their families, and utilize their resources in the most efficient way.

One example that shows how important it is to be prepared is a recent event that we have all experienced. At the beginning of 2020, the world was hit by the Covid-19 pandemic. Because of the announcement of a lockdown, people panicked and flocked to stores to try and stock up on food and other supplies. Mass shortages occurred, and people were then faced with the fear of a virus *and* running out of food. This short-sighted approach to dealing with a crisis was the least efficient way to deal with the situation, and consequences took forth. For preppers who had been prepared to deal with this, panicking and running out to buy things wasn't so necessary. Preparing in advance allows less disruption when crises come. These kinds of events truly make us realize the need to prep.

We understand that prepping can be an arduous activity and that the thought of going off the grid can be an uncertain and complex task. The very notion of leaving everything behind scares people because they have no idea at first what to expect. In a society dependent on the government to care for the people's every need, many might doubt if they would be able to survive at all without being closely linked to government-provided services. We also understand that you, the reader, may still be a beginner and think that you don't have the necessary skills to be able to survive in wilderness situations and that the thought of such cases can sound frightening. Or maybe you're a camping or survivalist enthusiast, and you want to leap at the chance of becoming more independent and getting out of the stress of the city. Whatever your station in life is, this book aims to provide the answers for you. This book is the perfect resource for anyone thinking of tackling the great outdoors. You'll learn about the first steps to living off the grid so that you can set up a sustainable off-grid home. You'll also receive tips and advice on how to protect yourself and your family in survival situations. Finally, if you're an experienced outdoor lover, you'll learn how to survive and thrive in nature, the place you treasure the most. Whatever problem you may be facing, this book aims to teach you one key skill: preparedness.

Other outdoor guides can seem confusing and restricted to only those with no experience having the right equipment, knowledge, or skills. These guides may not be as helpful to someone just starting to get into the prepper movement. Many guides seem to only focus on the countryside or wilderness survival. Fewer of them seem to deal with the need to survive in the urban environment, which is just as important because many emergencies can happen even if you're not outdoors. Prepping is for all times and all seasons. This guide aims to give you a truly holistic view of the topic of prepping. We won't assume that you're an expert in this sort of thing, and we'll start with the beginning by laying out the foundational concepts and give a plan of action. We also won't assume that you have access to expensive forms of equipment, so we'll show you how you can make use of the most basic of tools to live in an efficient and environmentally friendly way.

So, what kind of topics does this book cover? First, we'll give you the facts on the most crucial survival skills, what these survival abilities mean, how to learn these skills, and which real-life situations in which these skills can be best used. Then, we'll guide you to using these same skills in an urban environment and in the wilderness. Each step-by-step plan will be presented in an easy-to-read and practical fashion. Next, we'll explain to you all of the possible situations that you might need to prep for and how best to employ the skills learned in this book in such cases. This book covers the basics of survival 101, how to find water in hostile environments, finding food, and how to stay warm during the night in frigid conditions. We'll also discuss how to administer first aid, take care of yourself in the city and the wild. Lastly, we'll also help guide you in building shelters for various kinds of environments and using different kinds of tools and materials. However, the most important skill that this book will teach is how to develop the mindset of a survivor. What you do when you find yourself in perilous situations is important, but the mentality that you'll need for it is the backbone for all your plans. Preparing yourself mentally is possibly the most vital skill you can master in this life. It will see you through many scrapes and pitfalls. Developing a can-do attitude allows you to take the initiative and control situations rather than be controlled by them.

Who is Small Footprint Press?

"Accelerating Sustainable Survival for the Individual and our Planet"

"Prepping to survive a global catastrophe goes hand-in-hand with stopping the destruction of our planet by living sustainably!" Small Footprint Press Company Values.

While we aren't doomers who focus solely on disasters and collapses or on beliefs that the end of the world is nearing, we do believe in being prepared for the worst while living your best life each day. For this reason, we work toward promoting and encouraging sustainable, prepared living as an individual. While we guide individuals on prepping, we also teach the importance of living sustainably and self-sufficiently. Did you know that in 2021 over 45 percent of Americans, both men, and women, are invested in prepping for worst-case scenarios? (Laycock & Choi, 2021) We're not just talking about stockpiling food and toilet paper, but also equipment and taking instructional courses. It is only by realizing the fragility of the planet we inhabit that we can begin to develop the right attitude towards it. The future of the world as we know it is in our hands. We have to take steps to be prepared for any and every eventuality, and this book is the perfect starting point for that. The knowledge in this book is not intended solely as a guide for when you find yourself in those situations, but more a guide to being prepared for the situations you might find yourself in in the future.

Who is this book for?

This book is for men and women of all ages who want to have a hand in the destiny of our planet. It is for individuals concerned with the current state of the environment and who seek to make a tangible difference in their lives and the futures of everyone who lives on planet earth. Those who desire self-sufficiency and freedom from the government will love this book because it teaches the skills needed in order to be independent. Those from all walks of life are welcome to take the "independence challenge" and free themselves from the restrictions of modern life. Throughout your journey, this book will be your constant companion.

Chapter 1
The Basics of Survival

In light of the current world situation politically, economically, and in every other way, it is vital to have an understanding of the basics surrounding survival techniques. When difficult situations arise, as they often do, only those who are prepared will be able to not only survive but thrive in such situations. In order to build a framework for survival knowledge, you need to be able to educate yourself on the basic techniques first. To understand why wilderness survival is so important, you first have to understand the world you live in and the environment that is around you. Understanding the basics of survival is the first step to becoming truly independent in every area of your life and not have to rely entirely on governmental forces and establishments. So, while many think of prepping as being all doom and gloom, the opposite remains true. It is a chance to truly experience independence and finally enjoy present life, being prepared for the worst-case scenarios.

Why does Wilderness Survival Matter?

In the comfortable urban environment that many people find themselves in, survival is not a priority because they have access to everything they need when they need it. There is no need to take unnecessary risks to obtain rewards, in other words. Society has conditioned people into not having to fight for what they want. They are far too reliant on the government. However, unless we're planning on not living on Earth in the next few years, it would seem like a wise idea to learn these basic survival techniques. Before the advent of technology, humans always knew how to survive on what they had and often made do with little in the way of resources. These days,

6

this is no longer a consideration. But life is unpredictable. The best way to safeguard ourselves and our loved ones for the future is by developing our skills in the area of survival and encouraging those we know and love to do the same.

A crucial reason why survival skills matter is because of the constant change of our climate. Climate change is a latent threat that cannot be ignored for much longer. When the crises caused by this climate change come, our response will be proportionate to how much we've prepared for these moments. In order to combat the devastating situations caused by climate change, it would be wise to create a climate change response plan. This climate change action could be part of a much larger movement towards disconnecting from harmful practices that affect the environment. Think of it as a way to free yourself from the constraints of being connected to the grid so you can explore a new life. This book offers hope from the doom and gloom of the constant news we see each day. With the right mindset and plan, you can find freedom in being self-sufficient and ready.

How Does the World Respond to the Danger of Climate Change?

The globe is vast, and there are many cities in it. Each of these cities produces carbon emissions that affect the climate in some way, to a greater or lesser degree. A large number of people live in these coastal cities. Due to the rising sea levels, large numbers of these people will have to relocate, and the only way they can go is inland. However, there may be many more ways that people displaced can live. Newer innovations such as environmentally restorative communities are being created, even as we speak. These communities are being considered possible living spaces in the future by those who inhabit smaller islands because their homes may cease to exist in the future. These communities consist of a bunch of interconnected houses on floating platforms connected by small bridges and which contain gardens. On top of each roof is a green roof, or a type of vegetation positioned over a layer of waterproofing. But, how does all of this tie into the idea of creating a climate change disaster plan? The notion that there are innovations being thought of points towards the fact that there are climate change disaster plans being formulated. This planning can be applied to the individual. What can we do to develop sustainable plans for the future in our own lives and families?

As a start, it's important to know that there are different kinds of survivalists. Some are the typical preppers you sometimes see portrayed in the media as the gun-hoarding, food-stockpiling, disaster-predicting type. Next, there are those who take the job a little more seriously. Those who are farmers are technologically advanced and have methods of survival, which include open-source plans for every single kind of machinery and equipment that they need. Finally, there are those who have a simpler mentality: they believe that survival is just about survival and are quite happy to make use of as little or as much as they need in order to get by. What kind of plan you want to create depends on what your goals are. If you just want to live in a more environmentally friendly way, there are many ways to start planning to do this. The first thing you need to understand is how to survive in the wilderness. This involves a fundamental grasp of what bushcraft means. There is a real difference between what bushcraft means and what survival skills mean. Survival methods, or skills, refer to the ways in which you deal with difficult and unexpected emergencies when you are forced to fend for yourself. The goal in any survival situation is to make your way to safety. Bushcraft is an often voluntary exercise that requires you to make use of nature to sustain yourself for long periods. For example, someone practicing bushcraft might take a long period of time out in the woods and live on nothing but the land. On the other hand, someone who is in a survival situation might have been dropped there in a plane crash and have no means of immediate escape from the situation. The difference between survival skills and bushcraft are the types of situations and the urgency of these situations to a large degree. Let us examine bushcraft in more detail.

What is Bushcraft?

There are three main things you cannot survive without, no matter where you may find yourself. These things are well-known: water, food, and shelter. If you take two or even just one of these things away, your chance of survival drops from poor to none at all. Fortunately, there are courses that you can take that can help you to gain the skills you need to be more prepared in case you ever end up in a situation without the most basic necessities. Engaging in bushcraft activities is a great way to ensure that you get the type of mental and physical preparation you need in order to prepare for the most extreme of situations. Bushcraft mainly deals with the techniques you need to survive, but what if you are intending on spending a longer period of time in the wilderness? You'll need to pick up other skills that will help you to grow beyond just the three basic needs. These skills can also be incorporated into the term "learning bushcraft," This is also where bushcraft and survival skills tend to diverge. Survival skills are a lot more restrictive in terms of the fact that they are limited to a specific set of circumstances. On the other hand, bushcraft tends to think of the more long-term practicalities of being in the wilderness, and the amount of things that need to be learned is much greater as a result. There is a greater urgency with survival skills. There are necessities that cannot be ignored. With bushcraft, the pace of the whole experience is slower and can be seen as a learning experience rather than a life and death struggle. There are, however, specific skills that are common to both kinds of experiences. Let us look at some of these skills. They may vary in significance depending on the urgency of the situation and the context surrounding the person engaging in these skills and activities.

Tools

In order to survive in the wild, you'll need to learn how to use specific tools. These tools can give you access to the resources you need to not only survive but live comfortably. Some tools are limited in their use and are therefore only useful for extreme survival situations. Other tools are not as vital but are useful and helpful to have in order to make living easier. Whatever your needs may be, you'll need to be able to use the tools that you have at your disposal and sometimes even make your own in order to survive. In addition, learning to use tools will make you more independent.

Fire

The second skill you'll need to possess is the ability to make fire. Fire is unquestionably one of the most significant challenges that many survivalists face in extreme situations. You need to be aware of the different methods to create a fire depending on where you are and the tools that are available to you. The challenge in creating fire is not just in having the proper materials, but in that, you also need the right skills to be able to get it started. The climate and the wood's condition also have to be suitable to get a fire going. These things might not necessarily be in your control, so a lot of what you need requires the circumstances to be in your favor. You can, however, control how you use these circumstances to your advantage. Skills you'll need when building a fire include the following:

- Finding and stacking tinder
- Collecting and preparing wood
- Building a fire-making tool
- Building a fire pit
- Making and utilizing different kinds of fire for specific purposes

Not all fire is used as a heating device. Sometimes, it is constructed for other purposes. You will need to be aware of what these purposes are and how to best make use of them when the situation arises.

Shelter

Constructing a shelter takes knowledge of what materials to use and how to put these materials together in a way that makes a place where you can stay warm and dry and protected from the elements and dangers. It is vital to have skills in shelter building because without them, you could perish from the bad weather or freezing temperatures in a matter of hours. Here are the skills you'll need in order to build a shelter include the following: knowledge of woodcraft and woodworking skills, harvesting other materials, thatch weaving, making knots, making waterproofing, and more. For cold climates where there is actual ice and snow, you'll need to be able to make use of the snow to create your shelter, which requires a set of skills and knowledge all on its own. Depending on the situation you find yourself in, you'll have to learn to construct shelters of varying degrees of complexity. In an off-grid situation, you'll need to plan before you can build a shelter.

Water

Without water, you will perish. This is an absolute certainty, and thus the need for water takes precedence over everything else. When you find yourself in a difficult situation, you need to stop and think about where you can find vital resources. Knowledge of where to begin and how you're going to exploit these resources are critical to being prepared. What will you do if the traditional sources of water such as springs, lakes, and rivers aren't available? How will you purify water once you've found it? What will you do to make it drinkable? Such skills can only come through educating yourself. The skills you'll need include the following: water identification, water purification skills, making filters, building a fire, and creating containers for storing your water.

Food

Food is secondary when it comes to water, but it is still critical for you to find. Without food, you could perish in a few days. Food gives you the energy to keep moving. Without it, in any survival situation, you could easily fade out and die. Knowing where to find food and what is edible is not always common knowledge. People in survival situations know they have to eat, but they often lack the knowledge of what plants are safe to ingest and what animals are fit for consumption. For example, you may want to fish for food, but do you know the best way to do this? Where are the best places to fish in the river, for example? Is fishing done only with a line and reel, or are there other ways? This guide aims to help you discover more about how you can gather, safely prepare, and eat in all kinds of extreme situations. These are skills you'll need to be able to find food: foraging, hunting skills, the ability to fish and to create traps that can catch fish, the ability to capture small animals to eat, cleaning and cooking game, tracking game, and using scent concealers, use of different weapons to trap prey, and many more.

Navigation

If you're in an emergency situation and you want to find your way out of it, you'll need to be absolutely adept with your navigational skills. Finding your way from point A to point B isn't as simple as walking there. There are obstacles to overcome, and you definitely need to be sure you're heading the right way. The wilderness, combined with the shock and trauma of being lost, can be a disorienting place. You need to be mentally, physically, and emotionally prepared to plan ahead and figure out how you are going to get to safety. Your very life could depend on your ability to navigate using the tools you have. These tools aren't only the compass you have in your bag. Sometimes, you might have to rely on the sun and the stars to lead you. Having this knowledge tucked away can be a literal lifesaver.

First Aid

First aid is not only about applying quick and effective remedies to others; you also need it to save your own life. First aid is an absolutely necessary and critical skill. If you're wounded and lost, you'll need to first ensure that you remain alive so that you can access the resources you need in order to start planning your escape. Your good health is paramount at this point. And taking care of that health starts with being aware of first aid. Skills you'll need to be able to administer first aid, either to yourself or to others: the ability to do CPR, splint or stitch wounds, apply bandages, stop bleeding, make use of various kinds of plants and natural materials to attend to the sick, and many other skills.

All of these skills and more will be covered in further depth through future chapters. However, the main thing to realize is that this book is here to help layout all the things you need to gain your independence.

Survival Gear Checklist

Before you start your survival journey, you'll need to make sure you've got everything you need. The items on this list are primarily aimed at people who are interested in taking up bushcraft, but they can be applied in extreme emergency situations as well. If you know what items to use in these situations, you can make use of similar items when you find yourself in an emergency. Lack of preparedness can never be an excuse when faced with tough situations. Always prepare accordingly, and you'll put yourself in the best position to survive. The items on this list are divided into the different categories you're going to require them to be used. Sometimes, items will fit into more than one category. While you may not be able to carry everything on this list, you can try and approximate what you need based on the situation that you may find yourself in. You can begin to gather these materials months in advance if you're planning a trip. It is always good to have a kit that you can keep adding to before and when the situation demands it. It's important to realize that your *gear* can be collected in advance, but supplies will need to be gathered when necessary, as some things may not last. Always do your research on what you need. Always keep a kit available in your car and one in your home for emergencies.

Water filtration and purification items

To purify water and make it safe to drink, you'll require a mini water filter and water purification tablets. Together, these items can save you a nasty case of dysentery or an even worse waterborne illness while you're in the wilderness. Always be sure to take a water bottle with you. These can be used to store and water as you travel. A water bottle will be able to keep you hydrated while you're moving between sources of water. Make sure your bottle is made of metal so that it can be heated if you need to boil your water. In a world that is becoming increasingly water-scarce, proper conservation and treatment of water are also vital.

Shelters

Building your own shelter is a huge and critical step of the survival process. In order to create a livable shelter, you'll require a survival tarp or a piece of material that you can use as a cover. You can also invest in a tent that is easy to carry from place to place, and that can be easily installed. The disadvantage of a tent is that it can be heavy to carry, but it can serve you very well once it is set up. Hammocks are great if you're traveling in finer weather. They can also work in inclement weather and keep your body off the ground, something other sleeping arrangements might not be able to do. A hammock tent provides both the comfort of a hammock and the shelter of a survival tarp. These will tend to be more expensive. When all else fails, you can invest in a sleeping bag and an emergency blanket. These are relatively inexpensive and can be used in a pinch. Always be aware of the type of weather you might encounter before you start your survival journey and invest accordingly. Your shelter will depend on the type of climate you're in.

Weapons

When referring to weapons in a survival context, these are the things that you will need to use in the chance that you end up in a situation where you'll need to defend yourself. You would also be needing weapons that you can use to be able to hunt and fish. Finally, you're going to need weapons to use as tools, such as saws and axes. Let us look a little more closely at the types of tools you're going to need.

The first thing on your list is going to be a firearm, which is a sophisticated kind of weapon even at the best of times and requires some investment and expertise. If you're already trained, a firearm will be at the top of your list. Note that the ammo is considered survival supplies. There is no one size fits all approach to owning a firearm. However, when you're embarking on a survival mission, you'll want to choose the one that is light and efficient, as well as a weapon that is most reliable. You also need to make sure you have enough ammo to protect yourself, your family and to use for other tasks. If you're intending on hunting with your weapon, ensure that it is a weapon that has the ability to take down the caliber of prey that you want. Some kinds of weapons can be used for both self-defense and for hunting. Be sure to do your research before acquiring the type of weapon you want and also acquire the licenses that you might need. Bear in mind that you may or may not be able to simply discharge firearms at will. Be aware of the environments you find yourself in at all times.

Invest in a snake bore. A snake bore is a bore cleaner that is a must for anyone owning a firearm. Proper maintenance of your weapon is essential when you're in the wilderness. You'll need everything to function as it should.

You could also make your own weapons to use in the field. You can design and build these weapons as and when you need them while you're in the wilderness, but you may not have the materials and equipment you need. A better idea is to design what you need beforehand. Such customizable weapons include homemade knives, stun guns, and flamethrowers.

A bow and arrow is another essential item if you're planning on hunting. These weapons are perfect when stealth is required, and a firearm simply will not work. Their disadvantage is that they require some level of proficiency in order to operate properly, and conditions have to be optimal for their most effective use. Crossbows also fit into this category.

A tactical pen is also a weapon you might want to keep on your person. These are hardened metal pens with ink cartridges inside that are under pressure. They do not kill but can still be used to strike an opponent as a last resort. In addition, they are, of course, pens and can be used for making notes, maps, and many more helpful purposes.

Stun guns are useful for discharging a blast of electricity that will leave an opponent indisposed for a few moments. They are useful for self-defense only and are not 100% reliable. However, when they do work, they are perfect for situations where you're faced with imminent danger.

Mace spray is a substance that comes in small pressurized containers. It can be discharged at the faces of potential predators and enemies. It has a range of up to 20 feet.

In addition to these weapons, there are the usual spears, knives, machetes, saws, and other kinds of similar weapons you'll be needing to carry out tasks while you're on the trail.

Fire Starting Kit

Fire starting is synonymous with survival in the wilderness. Your ability to get a fire started could be the difference between life and death. It's not enough to simply learn to start a fire. You'll need to be able to adapt to the conditions you'll find yourself in quickly. Bear in mind that sometimes you're going to need to start a fire in a downpour or when it's sleeting or snowing. How will you preserve the integrity of your fire-making materials? Where will you find dry tinder or wood? Such knowledge has to be obtained before heading out on the trail. You'll need a lighter that works in all kinds of weather conditions. It is worth investing in a good one.

You could also invest in a ferro rod. This is a small device that requires no gas and is good for nearly 12,000 uses. It is also extremely reliable for creating a spark. They require a small amount of practice to use but are otherwise an extremely valuable addition to your survival kit.

Matches are useful to have around, but they are susceptible to getting wet in difficult conditions and can be rendered useless. However, you can purchase the waterproof variety that has some degree of durability in unfavorable conditions.

You can purchase something known as fire laces. These are shoelace-like items that have ferro rods attached to the end of them. These are easy to carry because you can thread them into your shoes, and you'll always have access to fire-making materials no matter where you are.

If you really want to start a fire, however, you're going to be relying heavily on a tinder box. Having access to dry tinder will always help you start a fire, no matter the conditions you find yourself in. In addition, some tinderboxes have built-in graters that you can use to break down dry wood so that it is easily usable as tinder.

Bladed Tools

A survival shovel is a tool used for displacing dirt, digging holes and trenches, and clearing the ground so that you can establish a campsite. It is a versatile and necessary tool and will perform tasks that you cannot do with a knife, for example.

A survival knife is a fixed-bladed implement that you will need to cut through stubborn items. It is an essential part of your survival kit. Be sure to invest in a knife that is durable and weatherproof.

An axe is a versatile tool that can be used for cutting down trees, cutting through branches, and for self-defense purposes. In a pinch, they can be used for hunting. Survival hatchets are another kind of survival axe but smaller.

A multitool is a device that has many different functions. Some are shaped like knives and have pliers attached to them. These pliers are very useful when you're in a situation where you need to remove objects or items that you can't grip with your fingers. These tools also have other bladed tools attached to them, like bottle openers, corkscrews, and other small bladed implements.

A multipurpose credit card tool is a tool shaped like a credit card that can be opened to reveal various useful items, such as knives and picks. These don't typically come with a set of pliers attached, but they are lightweight and versatile nonetheless.

Blade sharpeners are a must if you're planning on spending an extended amount of time in the wilderness. Your knives are your most important tools. They need to be cared for, and learning how to sharpen a knife and actually sharpening it are necessary skills. If your blade is blunt and unable to perform the purpose of which it is intended, it can put you at risk. Always take care of your tools.

Rescue Items

When you're in the wilderness, and you're seeking rescue, you need to have specific tools that will help you attract attention and possibly save your life. Unfortunately, in many instances, you will eventually have to improvise in your use of these tools.

Whistle

A signal whistle makes a sound that can be heard from a long way off, and it can draw attention to your plight. If someone is in the area, they might not be able to see your signal, but they could possibly hear it if it is loud enough.

Signal Mirror

A signal mirror is a mirror used to reflect the light of the sun onto specific objects. These are effective at being seen from many miles away.

Colorful items

If you don't have these items, you can improvise by creating a fire or by using colorful items, such as brightly colored clothing to attract attention. Discarded parachutes, for example, are often brightly colored and can be used to create eye-catching signals in a pinch. Always make sure that you keep fabrics and materials around with you if you find yourself in a survival situation.

Miscellaneous Survival Items

There are numerous other items that might be essential to your survival but are often overlooked. Depending on where you are, you might want to invest in fishing tackle. It is useful when you're attempting to fish and can be easily stored. You'll also want to have a flashlight on you. Tactical flashlights don't need batteries to be charged and can be priceless in a difficult situation, particularly if you're struggling to make a fire. Finally, consider investing in a survival pack in which you can keep all your smaller items. Other larger items can be carried on a tactical belt if you have one.

Survival Mentality

What is meant by a survival mentality? A survival mentality is the mindset of a winner in every situation that you find yourself in. It is the most important weapon in your arsenal, and in some situations, it could be the difference between life and death. So, why is a winner's mentality so important when you find yourself in a struggle for survival?

Planning and Preparation

First of all, a survival mentality helps you to remain positive in all circumstances. With this positivity comes confidence that you can carry out the tasks that you need to and that you can take the necessary steps in order to survive. Positivity breeds confidence, and confidence breeds success. In a life or death struggle, you need all the positivity you can get. If you have already cultivated this mindset, you're already on your way to coming out on top in any survival situation. You may not be able to predict the future, but you can always be mentally ready for it.

A strong mentality is one of self-reliance. The ability to do things for yourself and to be able to adapt to different situations is the mentality that you will need in many difficult situations. There are practical steps that you can take to make sure that you are able to cope with whatever comes your way.

The ability to be self-reliant comes from a quality that is inherent in all of us, but only some make use of it. It is the ability to plan and organize for the future. Proper planning is a sign that you have the mentality of a winner because you're able to put into practice the ideas that you have, you know that these ideas will work, and you're able to organize them in a coherent way.

Planning sometimes requires sacrifice, but those with a strong desire to win will be willing to put everything on the line in order to achieve their goals. The mentality of a winner doesn't only apply to survival situations. You need to have a never-say-die attitude in every aspect of life. You never know when you will require it.

Dealing With Anxiety

When you're out on the trail, there are times when you will start to feel overwhelmed by situations that you never thought you would encounter, no matter what your skill level in survivalism may be. We all get scared. This is a fact of life. But some people never appear to be rushed or concerned in any way. Why is this? It is because, a long time ago, they learned that whenever they're faced with a situation that threatens to derail their confidence, you have to remain outwardly and inwardly calm. This inner peace enables them to not panic in situations.

For the vast majority of us, though, fear is something that we don't generally tend to handle very well, like that the massive spider in the bathroom that causes us to lose our cool or a large, frightening, and noisy dog for some people. These are relatively minor disturbances. But when we're lost in the jungle, the threat is suddenly made more real in a disorienting and claustrophobic environment. Death can often occur in a matter of hours unless you're able to keep it together and take the necessary steps to extricate yourself from the predicament. So, how do we overcome fear in simple terms?

The first step is to identify the source of the anxiety. What is causing you to lose your mental focus at that moment? Let's take one hypothetical example: you're lost, there's a predator near you in the forest, and you know it's a wolf (even if you can't see it). Once you've identified that it is a wolf, the next step is to determine whether the fear is a rational or irrational fear. In the case of a wolf, the fear is most certainly rational and, therefore, a security feature in your mind. It stops you from going near that wolf instead of leading you into a panic. With the knowledge you now have, you're able to make a detour around the area where the wolf is, and you can avoid the danger. This is how fear works. We need to harness it to make ourselves stronger.

Our bodies are a cocktail of different chemicals, and when someone is stressed, certain hormones are pumped into the body. When we're in the grip of these hormones, they can affect how we react to situations. If we react negatively, we could end up making a situation that endangers ourselves or others. The key is to harness this fear and use it to our advantage.

The next step is to latch onto something bigger than ourselves. What drives us to succeed? What are some times when we've faced similar situations and overcome them? What are some times when we've faced situations and gotten through them, even though we didn't think we could? Latch onto these former times and remind yourself of what you're capable of and who you truly are. Then, you can do what you set your mind to. Activate your faith, whatever that may be to you. Remember a loved one. Harness the power of your emotions to take control of yourself, and thus your situation.

Survival Mindset Traits

There are certain traits within someone that's a survivor compared to a person who is not. In fact, we can all survive if we choose to change our attitudes towards life and towards our circumstances. Tenacity, adaptability, work ethic, creativity, positivity, acceptance, humor, bravery, and motivation are some of the qualities you need in order to effectively cope with the situations you find yourself in on a day-to-day basis. Let's look at a few of these traits.

Tenacity

Tenacity is the ability to remain steadfast even in the midst of difficulty. Tenacity has nothing to do with your physical fortitude or even your state of mind sometimes. It is a manifestation of your will to overcome any and every situation. Tenacity is fighting against your own desire to give up, even when this would seem easier than carrying on. However, tenacity alone is hard to maintain when the struggles of life are constantly beating you down. Guilt, fatigue, stress, anxiety, fear, and worry can all gnaw away at your inner strength. You have to maintain this inner strength throughout your ordeal. Talking to others can help if you're in a position where you're stranded with others. If you're on your own, this is more difficult. Invent distractions as a way of keeping your mind busy.

Adaptability

Adaptability is the ability to evolve according to changing situations and seasons and change the way you think and feel. In survival terms, this means, for example, that you won't act the same way in a forest as you will in a jungle. They are different environments and require different ways of operating. Having the knowledge and skills to be able to function in every kind of climate, weather, situation, or biome is known as being adaptable. Obstacles to your adaptability can be stubbornness and resistance to change. The way you can overcome this is by opening up your mind to different possibilities and solutions.

Work Ethic

Work ethic is a mental quality as well as a physical one. The desire to work hard starts in your mind. Survival is about hard work. In order to keep yourself alive, you have to work hard at performing the tasks that you need to perform. The downside is that you can often be hindered in your desire to work by things like circumstance, bodily injury, and factors beyond your control. Sometimes, there is nothing else to do in such situations, but to the best you can until circumstances are more favorable again. You may want to build a sophisticated and warm shelter, but it might be raining and impossible to do anything. The only option left to you might be to hide in a cave and wait out the rain. Such is the need for adaptability when you cannot perform the work that you really want to do.

Creativity

Creativity is a quality that allows you to think outside of the box. Hindrances to creativity might be fear of getting something wrong if you take a step outside the box. The way to overcome this is to get over your fear of failure. When you're in a life or death situation, you need to think of new ways to overcome difficult situations.

Positivity

Positivity is an overlooked quality when you're in a tense struggle for survival. All your effort might be so focused on getting through the experience that you forget to be thankful for what you already have. When you have a positive and determined attitude, difficult situations seem easier.

Acceptance

Acceptance of circumstances doesn't mean you accept their difficulties as well. It means that you acknowledge where you are at and are willing to make the necessary changes to get out of the situation.

Humor

Humor isn't just for clowns. Humor in difficult situations can actually be a beneficial thing because it helps you to view your situation from another perspective. Sometimes, it can be healthy to laugh, even when things seem dire. It allows you to rest for a bit when things get really tough.

Bravery

Bravery is not the absence of fear but the strength to overcome what is causing it, even when every part of your being is telling you that you won't be able to make it. Bravery can come in many forms. In survival situations, it takes on the form of choosing to fight for your life when it would be much easier to give up. Bravery never backs down from a fight.

Motivation

Finally, we all need motivation. Motivation is the desire to carry on even when there seems to be no hope. It is a skill cultivated by pushing yourself to complete tasks even when you feel tired. It is the glue that holds your survival together. It can sustain you long after other tried and trusted methods have failed. Never give up hope.

Chapter 2
Water: Where to Find It and How to Use It

It is a known fact that without water, humans will die after a very short period in the wilderness. Therefore, water is simply essential for basic human needs and cannot be ignored. The Rule of Three suggests the following theories.

Rule of Three divides significant aspects of survival into multiples of three. For example, humans cannot live for three minutes without air. You cannot live for three days without water, nor three weeks without food.

If you're in a group, you'll need to ration water according to how long your journey will be versus how many people are on the team. If it's just you, the situation becomes more straightforward. The key to water management is conservation. It would be best if you showed that you could plan ahead for several days and keep your supply going until the moment that you can be rescued. But first, you need to find and prepare the water, depending on where it is.

Where you can obtain water is mainly dependent on where you are in the world. Water is not readily available in the desert and thus must be carried along before entering the area. In the jungle, there are no such shortages. However, water may not be drinkable due to it being toxic, polluted, or filled with dirt or sand. If these issues are the case, then you'll need to bring a filter with you so that the water can be drinkable. In addition, you can make use of water purification tablets. Both of these things are necessary. But, in order to avoid putting the cart before the horse, let us look at the way in which you can procure water.

Finding Water

Water can come from many sources. The most common of these are rain, snow, lakes, rivers, and ponds. No matter where you are in the world, there should always be water available. Start by making sure you aren't wasting the water that you already have. Next, seek out other available sources of water. Remember, sometimes sources aren't apparent to the untrained eye. You will need to do your research before you find yourself in these situations so that you're able to find water when the time comes. The first thing you need to do is to be aware of the most common sources of water. These are areas that you can see and can easily access. Let us look at some of these areas.

Many people wonder if they should drink water at all if it is not clean or purified. The truth of the matter is that you will die a lot more quickly from dehydration than you would from water-borne diseases. Sometimes you have to make a choice on the spur of the moment. The best course of action, though, is to always look after your health. If you're prepared in advance, you stand less chance of finding yourself in these situations.

When you find a source of water, always assess it before drinking. Where is it situated? If it's a stream, does it flow downhill? If so, there may be contaminants further upstream that you're unaware of. For example, rotting animal carcasses and other waste can all contaminate water and make it unsafe to drink. Always purify and boil your water if you're able to. Never assume that water is safe to drink unless you can identify and know it is completely drinkable. With that being said, valleys are a great place to find water because water always flows downhill. You can use this to your advantage.

Lakes, Ponds, Streams, and Rivers

Always look for the most obvious forms of water first. When you find these sources, take a look at the color of the water. Dark, opaque colored, and still or slow-moving water is stagnant and might not be safe to drink. Water that has chemicals will have an unnatural hue and is definitely unsafe to drink. Water with chemicals in it cannot be made safe by purifying and boiling it.

Puddles

Water can be found in small depressions in the ground that collect rainwater and runoff water after storms and rain showers. You can also find this water pooled in crevices in rocks and caves, as well as in the hollows of trees. Don't drink water found in trees that are poisonous. Always assess the water in puddles for signs of life and algae. If there is significant microscopic life living there, move on to other sources.

Rain

Rainwater is the best source of water you can find if you are lucky enough to have a shower. Unless rainwater has run off another surface on its way to the ground, it is perfectly safe to drink and is purer than other forms of water. Collecting rainwater can be done in many ways: through using plastic pots, using clothing items to collect water and many other methods of collection.

Digging a Hole

Digging a hole can sometimes yield water if you dig in the right spot. If sand is wet or if you can perceive water under the surface, you can dig down to reach it. Let the water slowly fill up the hole. If you're at the coast, dig on elevated ground in order to avoid accessing saltwater. Digging near patches of vegetation can sometimes yield a good amount of water if you dig to the right depth.

Dew

If there are known dew in the area, you can access this if you construct a dew trap. Dig a small hole in the ground and place a cup at the bottom. Cover the hole with clear plastic, secure the plastic in place, and you should be able to harvest some of the dew in this way. You can also lay a cloth on the ground to collect some of the water. Make sure to wring it out at dawn before the sun comes up, or the water will evaporate and be lost. Dew traps don't typically yield the most water. However, if the dew is reliable, it is an efficient way to get some water.

Distill Water

You can distill water in various ways, namely in a solar still or by boiling. If your water is undrinkable, place it in a pot over the fire. Boil the water using a cloth placed over the container the water is in. The steam will be caught in the cloth, and you can then wring it out and use it. A solar still can also be useful. Start by digging a hole in the ground somewhere where the sun's rays can strike it and reach the bottom of the hole. Place a few green leaves or some vegetation in the hole. Add a collection container at the bottom and cover the hole with a piece of clear plastic. Place a small rock or stone in the middle of the place directly over the top of the collection container. As the temperature of the hole heats up, moisture from the vegetation inside should start to condense on the plastic, dripping down towards the container.

Water from Plants

Plants are a great source of water as they store it in their leaves, roots, and fruits. However, knowing which plants to take water from can be tricky. Some contain water within their stems and shoots, such as bamboo. Others, such as different kinds of trees, contain water within their roots. Grate or grind up chips of wood from the roots of the trees until it is pulp. As the water seeps out, catch it using a container. Some tree roots might give more water than others.

The aforementioned bamboo is one of the best natural sources of water you can find and should be used at every available opportunity if it is present in the environment. When you find it, look for the thicker stems that sound like they have water inside them. These will usually be hollow. Make a notch about four inches above the joint in the stem and collect the water that runs out of it. You can use this water without having to worry about purifying it as it will be fresh.

Cacti are another fantastic source of water and are probably one of the best-known sources of water. There are many different kinds of cacti, all of which grow in harsh and dry environments. Not all cacti can be used for water, however. The great Saguaro cactus of Northern and Central America, for example, contains liquid that is toxic. All cacti contain milky fluid that must be avoided, except for specific varieties. Cut the cactus open so that the inner flesh is exposed and suck out the liquid. You can also make pulp with the interior of the cactus by mixing up the flesh inside, as this will produce more water. However, this should be avoided as it can kill the plant. Always try to respect the environment, even if you are in dire need of water.

You can collect water from plants in indirect ways, such as condensation. Simply place a bag over the top of a plant and tightly seal it by the stem. In a while, if there is sunlight, you'll see water droplets start to form on the surface of the bag. You can use this water immediately as it is perfectly fresh and safe to drink.

Sea Water

Seawater cannot be drunk immediately as it contains too much salt. It will poison you if you drink more than even a tiny amount, as it changes the pH of your blood and causes organs to stop functioning the way they should. Seawater must be distilled to remove the salt, but this is a laborious process for little reward. If you find yourself in a desert island survival situation, it may be tempting to take huge gulps of seawater when nothing else is available. However, this is a fatal mistake. Allow your common sense to take over, and instead, carefully gather water in other ways. These ways won't make you sick and won't lead to lethal complications.

Other Signs of Water

Vegetation is one of the biggest indicators that water is nearby. Clusters of trees, bushes, and plants are surefire signs that water is at least below the surface of the Earth there and that water has been in that region in the recent past. Look for signs on the earth that water flowed there. Valleys, where there are bunches of trees, are great places to find water. A lesser-known way of finding out where water is is to look at the sky. The patch of sky over a water source will often appear bluer than the rest of the sky. In addition, dawn is a great time to look for water. Fog and mist tend to congregate over water sources.

Wildlife Indicators

One of the most common ways to track water sources is to look for animal spoor or footprints. However, these are not the only ways that you can make use of animals to find water sources. First, look for signs of animal waste. They will invariably point to water sources since many animals leave their waste near sources of water. Birds are another excellent indicator that water is nearby. Low-flying, grain-eating birds could be an indicator of water. The presence of enormous swarms of insects inside cavities such as a tree trunk could be an indicator that water is inside. You can use a plastic tube to siphon the water out of these cavities. Finally, use your ears and listen for the presence of water-dwelling animals, such as frogs and toads. They can lead you to water sources if you can hear them in the distance, particularly at night. All you have to do is follow the sound.

Unusual Water Sources

If you find yourself in a winter situation and snow and ice are on the ground, you can make use of these. However, before you get tempted to scoop up handfuls of snow, bear in mind that it will have to be boiled and purified as well. Depending on the climatic and environmental conditions, snow might contain impurities. You can melt snow over a fire, but you can use your body heat to do so in the absence of this. You can also make use of tree ice if snow is not a viable option. However, be careful of ingesting the water from tree ice if the environment is susceptible to pollution or there has been a recent nuclear fallout.

How to Determine Water Quality

There are numerous ways you can tell if the water in a specific area is safe to drink without even testing it. Obviously, you want to boil and purify all water if you can. But if you're in a hurry and you cannot wait, there are some indicators that can, at the very least, give you a sign that water is reasonably safe to ingest. These signs apply not only to the water but also to the environment that the water is in. Look at the types of animals that are living in the water. What kinds of animals are they? Certain kinds of frogs and fish will only live in water that is fresher. You can research what these specific animals are, but, in a more general sense, water that is teeming with healthy aquatic life is generally more fit for humans. Water that is covered in algae, muddy, green, or stinking is not generally water you want to ingest, even if you boil it and filter it. There are some chemicals and substances that can't be removed from the water so easily. Always ensure that you're able to trace the source of where your water comes from so that you can assess whether there are any contaminants in it.

Finding the Cleanest Source Possible

Realize that clear water doesn't necessarily mean that it is safe to drink. In prepping situations, you need to ensure that the sources of water you bring onto your property are clean and safe for you to drink. Make sure that the place you decide to pitch your survival home is close to sources that are not contaminated. Always look for sources of life in and around water sources. A lack of life means sources may be tainted. A green and algae-ridden stream may be putrid, but it means that there is life in the water. If taken and used, and prepared correctly, this water can be drunk once it is in a safe state. Always filter, boil and treat any and all wild sources of water, no matter how clean you think they may be. Always verify that there are no bacteria in the water by looking at the state of the area where it has come from. And finally, never assume it is safe before you try it.

Purifying Water

Once you've obtained water, the next step is to make it drinkable and safe for consumption. If you're using it for other purposes, it is not such a big deal if the water contains contaminants because these aren't getting into your system, i.e., if you're washing or bathing in it. But if you're drinking it, you need to take the utmost care. So, what are the ways you can purify your water and make it safe?

Boiling

One of these ways is by boiling it. Boiling gets rid of the impurities, but it doesn't get rid of the larger particles. If you're able to get a fire started, boiling is a relatively simple process:

1. Filter the water through a clean cloth.

2. Draw off the clear water.

3. Let it boil for about 3 minutes and leave it to cool before drinking it.

Water Purification Tablets

Water purification tablets are a valuable thing to have when you need to purify water in a hurry. They do not, however, remove particles from water. This can only be done through filtering. The best tablets to use when purifying your water are iodine tablets. These are cheap and easy to find. They do, however, leave a certain taste in the water. Different brands of tablets last longer than others. Always check the shelf life of the tablets you're buying. A product called *Potable Aqua* is one of the best products you can buy because it purifies water in a very short space of time, in about 35 minutes. When you don't have time, and you need to purify water in a hurry, this can be a great product to buy. However, if you have thyroid issues or allergies to shellfish, you might want to avoid using iodine if at all possible. Children also dislike its strong medicinal flavor.

Filtering

Filtering is a great way to get rid of particles, dirt, and insects from your water. It will also remove sand and grit. It is easy to set up because you can use natural materials, such as rocks and stones. Filtering water through sand itself will remove many of the impurities, but you will still need to boil it afterward. Create a cone out of leaves or twigs or some other kind of material and fill it with sand, small stones, or vegetation. Place a piece of material or fiber at the bottom of the cone before you do this to prevent your filtration material from leaching out. Boil and wash your cloth before using it as a filter.

Distillation

Distillation has already been addressed in some detail, but you should know a few more helpful things about it. Distillation is a technique used in the tropics and the Pacific, where the climate is humid. Often, you'll discover water in these locations that seem safe to drink, but it is, in reality, fairly bad for you because it contains large amounts of salt. One way you can get rid of this salt is through the process of distillation. As mentioned previously, you need a container and a source of heat. Heat the water in the container with a cloth over the opening of the container. As the steam rises, it will be trapped in the fibers of the cloth, which you can later wring out and use. The residue from the water should be left behind.

Chemicals

You can use chemicals to purify your water, such as bleach, but this process should be approached with great care. Bleach is among the most common disinfectants used to purify water. A few drops are sufficient to purify a moderate amount of water. After adding the bleach to the water:

1. Put the cap back on your bottle and turn it upside down, unloosening the cap, so a little of the bleachy water gets out onto the rim of the bottle.

2. Allow some of the water to get onto the outside of the bottle as well.

3. Leave the bottle in a cool, dark place for about 30 minutes.

It should taste like chlorine and be perfectly safe to drink.

Plants

You can make use of various kinds of plants to purify your water. Banana peels and fruit peels are among some of the most accessible plant materials that you can use. Place the water in a bag or container and tightly seal it with the type of plant material that you want inside. Chemicals within the plant itself will naturally disinfect the water. Be extremely cautious if you're in the wilderness and you don't know what specific plants are present. Some could be deadly poisonous and should be avoided at all costs.

Build Your Own Filter

You can construct your own water filter using a few bits of wood and some flexible hose and glue. It is a straightforward project that will really help out if you're in a pinch. A piece of PVC pipe is attached to a water source, and glue or epoxy is used to secure the wood inside the tube. Water is then passed through the tube and filtered through the wood on its way to the container or receptacle you are using. This is a great way to filter your water, and it is safer than some other methods.

Now, when living in a prepper situation, you're going to have constant sources of water flowing through or near your property, or you should have if you have chosen the right location for your home. Depending on the way you have chosen to set up your water purification system, you're going to need to keep other methods on hand for emergencies. This is part of your long-term planning phase. One of the best ways to prep for water purification emergencies is to keep a steripen. They are small and easy to use, and they can prep up to 8,000 liters of water. This is a tremendous amount for something so small. They should be an integral part of any prepper's arsenal.

Chapter 3
Don't Starve: Finding Food in the Wild

The Importance of Food

Food is the next most important element in your survival journey. Without it, you can't hope to stand the rigors of the environment, and it provides the much-needed energy and sustenance in a harsh and unforgiving landscape. In this section of the guide, you'll learn about where to find the food that you need, what the best kinds of food are for you, and how to prepare such foods. It's important to be aware of how to cook and store food once you're in the wilderness. The knowledge contained in this chapter will allow you to pick out the right equipment before embarking on your survival journey.

Food provides energy, which is vital once you're on the trail. Without it, you could quickly fade away and not have the strength to do essential tasks that will help you to stay alive. Food provides a morale boost, and it is a great distraction from the difficulty of the situation that you find yourself in. Food is absolutely vital to life in the wild. It is of the utmost importance that you receive the vitamins and nutrients that your body needs to stay healthy and strong while in the wild.

The essence of hunting is to try and find the food that is the most accessible first. If you spend more energy hunting for food than the energy you will obtain from it, then your efforts are being wasted. Therefore, efficiency is key in the wild. Part of this efficiency consists of planning ahead so that you can be prepared for any kind of eventuality.

In an off-grid home situation, you'll need to plan ahead because you won't have access to meat at a butcher unless your home happens to be near a market. Therefore, you will need to know how to hunt, kill, prepare, and store meat so that it doesn't go bad. In addition, by storing said meat, you're saving up for the future.

Where to Find Food

Food of many different kinds is all around you. You just need to know the best places to find it based on the environment that you find yourself in. Let's look at some of the places you could encounter on your survival journey and how these differ in terms of the food you can expect to find and also how you can access it.

Wetlands

Wetlands are home to a huge variety of life because they contain large bodies of water, as the name suggests. In these bodies of water, you can find all kinds of life. Animals from all over the region come to drink at these water sources as well, and this means it is much easier to track and trap prey. Examples of these water sources in wetlands include ponds, lakes, streams, and rivers. You can find frogs, toads, fish, mollusks, crustaceans, and snails in these areas. In addition, aquatic life can be located in the muddy bottoms of these rivers, streams, and ponds.

Near the ocean, eating is even better. Various kinds of fish, crabs, mussels, clams, and seabirds all present an excellent opportunity to grab something to eat. Tidal pools are a fantastic way to find prey that is trapped when the tide goes out. Always be sure to be careful what you eat and ensure that it is not poisonous.

Valleys and Mountains

Inland areas can contain both mountainous, rocky regions, open fields, and forests. One of the most accessible sources of food you can come across in these regions is insects, such as grasshoppers, locusts, and crickets. Termites, ants, grubs, and other similar creatures can be found in rotting plant matter, logs, and vegetation. Frogs, salamanders, birds, eggs, and worms can also be eaten, but caution is needed with some kinds of frogs and salamanders that can be toxic to humans. Eating these kinds of animals won't cause you to gain weight or provide a sufficient amount of energy, but they will keep you alive in the short term. It is about making use of what you have when you are able to find it. There is no room for sentiment when you're faced with a potentially perilous survival situation.

Deserts

Food is typically harder to come by in arid regions due to the lack of water. Desert areas are more of a challenge to find any kind of protein source because there are fewer animals that live there due to the extreme dryness of the climate. Finding food in these regions can be a challenge at the best of times, and so you have to take what you can get when you can find it. However, there are certain kinds of animals that have found a way to exist in these regions, despite all odds. These include yak, various burrowing squirrels, and rabbits, among others. Snakes can and have been eaten in the desert. They are a good source of protein when there is little else to be found. Scorpions are also present. They may not present to be the most glamorous source of food, but they will help you to survive when there is nothing else. Be careful of hunting them. When you encounter one, hold it down with a sharp stick and remove the tail. Next, peel off the shells, and roast them over a fire. Insects and various kinds of burrowing lizards are also common in these regions. These can be treated the same way as you would the scorpion: split small lizards open, remove their internal organs and roast them over a fire with a sharp stick. There are numerous ways to prepare insects, which will be addressed later in this guide.

There are a number of key problems you might face when hunting for food in the desert, and it is best to be prepared for this. The first is that animals that live in these arid regions are often well-camouflaged and adapted to protect themselves if they are faced with danger. As a result, they are difficult to catch because they are well suited to a lifetime of avoiding capture by larger predators. The second issue is that time able to be spent hunting for food is limited because of the inhospitable climate.

Tips for Finding Food in the Wild

These are some helpful tips for finding food in the wild and strategies for planning your approach to finding food before you even embark on your survival journey.

The first tip you need to be aware of is to avoid brightly colored creatures, as these are colored in such a fashion as a warning to predators. These animals can contain bitter substances, toxic chemicals, or spines or hairs. They can also bite or sting. This does not mean that all brightly colored animals are dangerous, but that the vast majority are.

Before you go out, do your research thoroughly so that you know where to find food and what to expect in any survival situation. Although you might have the right equipment, this doesn't mean that you will be able to use it effectively. Therefore, you need to plan ahead thoroughly and use your knowledge wisely.

Carrying various guidebooks can be an invaluable help in survival scenarios. However, you might not know everything about the subjects you most require an understanding of. In these cases, you will need to get a book that helps you to access and use this knowledge on the spot. Great examples of these guides include plant guides and guides to different kinds of animals familiar to the region you will be traveling to. Plants, in particular, need special attention, as there are many varieties that look like each other. Educate yourself on plant identification before going into the wild.

Always remember that unless impossible, you need to cook all food thoroughly in order to eliminate pests and diseases. Cooking food also makes it more palatable and pleasant to eat. In addition, the warmth acquired from hot food can raise morale, so before you begin your survival journey, always be sure you know how you are going to generate heat and power so that you can cook your food thoroughly.

If you're going into the wild, you're going to need to know how to hunt and kill various forms of wildlife. While it would be nice to find food laid on, in the wild, the initiative is required in order to gain the food you need for eating. Therefore, you have to be prepared to trap, hunt, and catch animals, birds, and fish. Educate yourself on proper methods of trapping and the tools you'll need to take along with you in order to construct said traps.

In emergencies, you'll need to have this knowledge stored. What will you do if there is a sudden food shortage and the shelves are bare? Money will profit nothing. Only your knowledge of the wild will matter because you'll be equipped to take advantage of the conditions around you. Having a general understanding of how to find food starts with being prepared and being educated. With that being said, let's look at the most important foods that you will need to be going for and what you should be looking to hunt and eat based on your skill level in survival situations. Not everyone has the skill to go after the same food. Some people are more experienced. You should not spend unnecessary energy seeking after large game, for example, if you do not need to be doing that. Rather focus on things you are able to manage.

Pyramid of Wilderness Survival Food

What is the Pyramid of Wilderness Food?

Knowing what food you can and can't hunt for and trap in the wild is vital to ensure that you don't waste time going after the wrong kinds of prey. Doing so will result in wasted time and precious energy that you can't afford to lose in a precarious survival situation. So, to avoid this problem cropping up, there is a chart to help you plan your hunting, fishing, and trapping escapades. It is known as the pyramid of wilderness survival food. The pyramid categorizes your ability to hunt and catch prey based on your survival ability. This could save you time and also your life because you won't be going into situations you can't handle. In addition, this pyramid will explain the techniques used to obtain certain kinds of food, examples of the animals you will be looking for, and how to cook and prepare these foods.

When you first begin your survival journey, you'll be looking at the most basic of foods you can find. You'll be eating food that consists of slow-moving prey and animals that are harmless and easy to catch or food that doesn't move at all. These kinds of food include plants and insects.

As you become more skilled, you'll graduate to fish and faster-moving creatures. At your most skilled level, you'll be chasing and trapping quicker and larger prey in more complex survival situations. Some foods may seem strange to you, given their position on the pyramid. One of these foods you wouldn't expect to find high up on the pyramid is mushrooms. This is because mushrooms take a lot of skill to identify, and so they should be left to those preppers and survivalists who are more adept at identifying those that are safe to eat and those that aren't.

At the highest level, you'll not only learn to kill large game but to skin and prepare it as well. This requires a knowledge of how to prepare different kinds of meats in different situations.

Tiers of Wilderness Food

Large Game

Large game is right at the top of the pyramid, as it represents the most difficult prey to kill. It requires specific kinds of weaponry and more sophisticated traps than other forms of creatures. These animals are best left to expert survivalists. Examples of these kinds of animals are larger herding animals, such as elk, gnu, yak, caribou, deer, wild boar, and other similar creatures. Note that the animals on this list are not only reserved for the experts because of their size; they are also extremely dangerous if they are threatened. Hunting these creatures requires the use of a large caliber weapon that could draw unwanted attention to yourself. Hunting with silent weapons is difficult and requires patience. However, hunting and killing are only the beginning steps of the process. You need to know how to prepare, store, and carry the meat once it is killed.

Every species of animal is different, but for the most part, when you are faced with large game, you need to approach it in much the same fashion. First, make a small hole at the top of the breast and allow internal gasses to emit. Be prepared for a foul odor. Next, remove the entrails. Make an incision along the carcass to the pelvis and open up the abdominal cavity. Cut away the internal organs and put them in a bag if you're intending on keeping them. Do this as quickly as possible because entrails left inside the carcass could make the meat toxic. Try as much as possible to keep the meat in a cool place so that it degrades less quickly.

Turn the carcass upside down and allow the blood to drain out. Be sure not to let any waste matter from the animal to come into contact with the meat, as this can cause it to go sour. Next, remove the intestinal tract from the back of the animal and use the "hole" at the back end as a draining vent for internal juices.

When you want to cook and prepare larger animals, you'll need to be aware of how to set your cooking station up. Again, this should have already been thought about and prepared for before you even started hunting and killing specific kinds of game.

For cuts of meat from large animals, you will want to build a spit that can be used over a fire and rotated. There are various ways to do this. A green stick works well over an open fire. Affix the cut of meat to the stick and place it over the fire using two forked upright sticks to hold it in place. Turn the meat at intervals to keep it from burning. Alternatively, you can use a similar arrangement to hang a fireproof pot or another container above the fire, and you can boil your meat in stock or liquid. What you decide to do with it depends on the time you have and the resources you have available to you.

Smaller Game and Birds

Next on the tier list are birds and smaller game. These creatures are high up in the tier list because they are difficult to catch, and they require a certain amount of effort to trap and hunt down. They are, however, not as difficult as hunting the largest game. A lesser experienced hunter might have success with these animals, but it will require a considerable degree of survival and hunting skill. Knowledge of how to construct snares and traps is necessary in order to be successful at this level of hunting. Examples of the creatures you'll be hunting in this tier are quail, ducks, pigeons, geese, rabbits and hares, mice, squirrels, and similar creatures. Try to stay away from hunting creatures like weasels and badgers, as these animals are highly aggressive and could do more damage to you than you know before they die. Avoid potentially painful situations.

Prepare small game and birds by splitting them open down their belly and opening them out. Remove the entrails from these animals. Remove the feathers from birds and roast them whole without removing the bones. Save the heart and liver from these birds, as it makes good eating. When preparing pheasant, partridge, pigeon, grouse, quail, and other similar birds, leave them in a bucket of water for a few hours in order to drain the blood from them.

For small animals, like rabbits and muskrats, for example, you can hang them up by their legs in order to drain the blood. Make two small slits at the ankles and make two slits in the inner thighs that connect to the vent and throat of the animal. Pull off the skin and try to leave it as intact as possible. Open up the animal and remove the entrails, saving the heart and liver for later. In muskrat species, remove the scent glands from inside the animal, as this can taint the meat.

You can cook the birds or small game over a spit, or you can simply lay them on the hot coals. What you can do is to let the fire burn down until only hot coals are visible. Then take several green sticks and lay them on top of the coals. Place the birds or game on top of the coals and allow them to cook gently. You can even make kebabs using pieces of the meat. You can attach various kinds of vegetables and other meats to these kebabs.

Storing meat can be done through a process of salting and drying it. The first key thing to note is that meat needs to be stored in a cool and dark environment. Too much sunlight and warmth will proliferate the growth of bacteria in uncooked meat. Cooked meat can be stored for a short period of time without preservation, but it must be consumed as soon as possible after the animal is killed.

For longer-term storage, the meat will need to be sun-dried. First, trim off the fat and cut the meat into long strips. Hang these strips in the sun until they are black and hard. Meat can be kept in a bath of saltwater before this process in order to cure it. When eating dried meat, be sure to eat another kind of food alongside such, preferably something that contains fat in it. This will avoid you getting an upset stomach.

Other sources of nutrition you can gain from both small and large game are their bones, organs, and blood. This may not sound like the food you're used to in your urban environment because this is a different and altogether serious situation. When you're faced with life or death situations, you have to use every part of the animal, including the parts you might not be used to seeing.

Animal blood is a rich source of iron and many other nutrients. When an animal is draining, be sure to have a container ready to catch any blood you might want to use. To make it more palatable, add it to a broth or soup.

Bones are rich in minerals. You can grind them up, or you can add them to soups and stews as an accompaniment. Crack open large bones using a heavy object and extract the marrow from them. You can use this in many different ways, and it is highly nutritious.

Reptiles, Amphibians, and... Mushrooms?

The next on the tier list are reptiles, mushrooms, and amphibians. These creatures are slightly easier for survivalists to find and trap, but they still require a reasonable degree of hunting skill and definite knowledge of more than just the basics. Finally, mushrooms are high up on this list because specific knowledge is required in order to identify which are poisonous and which are edible. An inexperienced survivalist would not be able to identify these mushrooms with any degree of consistency.

Reptiles and amphibians can be split open and their insides removed. They can then be lightly charred over an open fire. Be careful of any poisonous varieties.

Amphibians can be caught using your bare hands. Frogs, toads, turtles, tortoises, and other similar creatures make great eating and are easy to catch. They can be cooked and roasted over a fire. Turtles can be boiled in their shells. Detach the shell before eating. Cut the heads of scorpions and snakes along with their stingers. Be extremely cautious when gathering certain varieties of frogs as these can be deadly poisonous.

Edible varieties of mushrooms can be eaten raw or cooked. They can be added to other dishes and make a great accompaniment to soups and stews. Each variety is unique in its texture and flavor. However, always be sure that the variety of mushrooms you choose is safe to consume. Do your research thoroughly before attempting to gather mushrooms from the wild.

Seafood and Eggs

The following creatures on the list are crustaceans, seafood, fish, and eggs. Eggs are easier to find since they don't run away when you try to catch them, but they still require a certain level of skill to safely remove them from their nests. Fish requires reasonable skill to catch, but it can be easily and quickly learned. More inexperienced survivalists will be able to handle these creatures when searching for food efficiently. All that is required is the knowledge of how to make fish and crustacean traps, the knowledge of where to look, and the knowledge of what kinds of fish and shellfish are safe and edible.

You can catch fish and other seafood by making a hook. Cut a piece of stick about 2 inches long and sharpen it at both ends. Hide the small fragment inside a piece of bait. When a fish swallows it, it will become lodged in its throats.

The way to prepare fish is by simply roasting them on the grill or splitting them down the middle, removing the backbone and entrails, and laying them over hot coals. Depending on the size of the fish, you might not need to even debone or clean them. This is the case, particularly with fish-like sprats. They don't need to be cleaned, only quickly roasted over hot coals and eaten as quickly as possible. You can, of course, gut these small fish if you wish, but they are often eaten as they are. For larger fish, you do need to gut them, but it is a relatively simple process. First, cut the fish from the tail side to the head on the belly side. Pick the fish up by the tail and remove the scales by scraping them off. Remove the bloodline and the kidneys from them.

For storage, you can dry the fillets of fish over a fire on low heat. Again, make use of some kind of material to make sure they don't get burned.

Mollusks require certain knowledge in being able to prepare them. Always bring a short, sharp knife with you if you're going to be trying to gather mussels, scallops, winkles, and similar creatures. These creatures survive by clinging tightly to rocks in shallow pools, and they need to be removed. Simply cut through the muscle holding the creature to its surface, and it should dislodge. In order to open bivalves, as this is what these are known as, cut through the hinge at the back of the creature, applying pressure to the point. Then, pry it open and extract the creature inside.

Insects

Insects themselves can be prepared by removing their spiny legs, wings, heads, and hard shells and only eating the body itself. For those who are squeamish about the idea of eating insects, a good way to make them more palatable is to grind them between two stones. Then, you can use their remains in other dishes, and you won't notice that you're eating them. Avoid eating poisonous or toxic insects, such as ticks and flies, as these can make you sick. These are valuable kinds of foods to come across, but you need some knowledge of which are edible. So, this tier is for those who are novices but who have taken a few steps down the road, as it were. It is not the most accessible tier because it still contains a level of skill when you're trapping and collecting insects.

Insects can be prepared in many different ways. Remove their heads, wings, outer carapaces, and legs, and impale them on sharp sticks before roasting them over the fire. Worms can be prepared by removing their guts and lightly roasting them. They can be soaked beforehand to get rid of any internal matter. Worms can also be eaten raw if desired. However, be careful with doing this as some can harbor parasites themselves. Do prior research on what can and can't be eaten.

Nuts, Seeds, and Grains

The second-largest tier of the pyramid contains the foods considered to be among the easiest to find, harvest, and collect. Unsurprisingly, this tier contains much of the food belonging to trees and plants. Fruit is on the list, as well as nuts and grains.

Nuts, seeds, and grains can be eaten raw or cooked. They do not need specific preparation other than removing the outer shells from certain varieties. Some kinds of nuts, such as acorns, need specific kinds of preparation before they can be eaten and should be avoided. But, for the most part, nuts and fruits make an easy and nutritious meal.

Plants and Berries

The last tier is the widest and therefore considered the easiest. These foods include berries, roots, tubers, flowers, and shoots. Finding these foods is an entry-level skill for survivalists and should not be too taxing. Some education is required, but by and large, if you're in this tier, you should stick to only eating the foods that you are able to collect and safely prepare. Fruit and other kinds of plants can be eaten raw for the most part.

Chapter 4
Staying Warm

Why Staying Warm is Important

Staying warm in colder weather is vital to survival when you're in the wilderness. There is no doubt at all about that. Cold weather, torrential rain, sleet, snow, and fog can all combine to ruin your morale. Therefore, it is vital that you have a plan of action for when this kind of weather comes along. You need to be prepared both mentally and physically to handle the rigors of climate. The way you stay prepared is by researching and understanding how to stay warm and dry even before you find yourself in such situations. When electricity and heating fail in urban environments, how will you keep yourself warm? You need to be already prepared for such an eventuality. Cold weather is not the only killer. Rain and floods can also prove potentially fatal. How will you deal with such events and ensure that you stay warm and dry?

The Dangers of Cold

Cold is not only damaging to morale, but it is also a killer blow to your health and wellness. Cold causes various functions in the body to stop working properly. It can further weaken a body already wracked by the pressures of life in the wilderness. Humans were meant to thrive and survive at optimum temperatures.

In order to effectively plan for all kinds of weather conditions, including cold, you'll need to be aware of what you can and can't bring along with you on a trip. You have only a certain amount of room, and therefore what is carried must have a specific purpose. The dangers of not preparing for freezing temperatures are manifold.

Your body will start to feel tired and sluggish at first. Your alertness will diminish, and your mind will feel less clear. Because you feel sluggish, you won't have the energy to get up and perform critical tasks that you need to survive, such as finding food or water.

Brain fog is another key danger of extremely cold temperatures. When the body cools down, your metabolism slows, and blood cools as well. As a result, less oxygen is imparted to the brain, and your thinking slows down as a result.

Shivering and shaking are one of the signs that the temperature within the body is too low and needs to be raised urgently. In addition, shivering can mean that you won't be able to carry out specific tasks that require you to be articulate, such as tying knots and other crucial skills.

Frostbite is the bane of those who find themselves mired in extremely cold conditions. When water molecules trapped within the body begin to freeze, it causes damage to internal organs, skills, and nerves, among others. It can even cause death in rare cases when decay and gangrene start to set in. The early stage of frostbite is called frostnip, and it is a warning that more severe problems are about to occur. Therefore, you should take measures to keep the affected part of the body as warm as possible when you begin to experience these symptoms. Usually, frostbite is most dangerous when it affects the body in conjunction with other symptoms.

The following are the signs of frostbite: numbness in the affected area, discoloration on the skin, a feeling of pins and needles, itchy or sweaty skin, or a clammy feeling, a loss of sensation to cold or heat, a hardening or lack of plasticity in the skin, pain, and soreness in the affected area, and other symptoms.

It is important to note that at first, your skin won't feel hardened at all, so this is not a reliable indicator of incoming frostbite.

When you notice these symptoms, the first thing you need to do is to try and keep the affected part warm as much as possible. Gently warming the area will help to alleviate the pain and inflammation.

Hypothermia is another nasty condition, which is well known to experienced survivalists. This infamous condition occurs when the body temperature drops below a certain level, and your bodily organs can't work properly as a result. Death can occur in a matter of hours if not treated. The body has an optimum running temperature, and falling below this temperature can be fatal in many circumstances.

Symptoms of hypothermia include the following: shivering, slurred speech, faint pulse, irregular breathing, trouble articulating sentences, poor coordination, memory loss and confusion, and eventual loss of consciousness. It is incredibly challenging to deal with hypothermia if you're alone because of the way in which it affects the body. Therefore, you need to be around people who can help you. Or even better, prepare for your survival experience and take the necessary steps to keep yourself warm. Let's start by looking at the most basic of needs when you're in the wilderness: the shelter itself.

The Need for Shelter

This section is not so much concerned about learning how to build a shelter in detail, as this will be addressed a bit later. Instead, it is concerned with the need to start preparing yourself by gathering the tools and materials you'll need before you start your journey and what knowledge you'll require in order to build an effective shelter. In short, it is about the strategies you'll require once you start planning for the long term.

Strategies for Dressing Properly and Shelter Building

Dressing For The Cold

Having looked at some of the dangers associated with cold weather, let's look at some of the ways in which we can get out of the cold.

The first strategy is to stay dry by any means necessary. The rule of thumb when you're in the wild is that moisture on your clothing or next to your person at any time is a definite no-no. Moisture destroys your equipment, food, tools, weapons, and clothing. In addition, it can make you uncomfortable and lead to rashes and skin conditions, which can be really distracting and frustrating when you're already in a difficult situation.

Dressing yourself correctly so that you make the best use of warm air pockets is a good way to stay warm in cold and wet conditions. This is done by layering clothing so that it wicks moisture away from your skin. Outer layers can be used for protection against the wind. Wear clothing with spaces in between the linings so that warm air circulating through the fabric from your body is trapped between the layers. In doing so, you'll keep yourself warmer than if you were just using simple fabrics, such as wool, for example.

Invest ahead of time in clothing that can keep you warm and dry. Think about what fabrics you'll need in order to create such clothing, in case you're unable to get any. For example, fur-lined jackets are a must if you live in an area where potentially cold weather is a common occurrence.

The buddy system is the means by which people who are in survival situations together keep each other warm and dry. It is always good to have someone with you when you're in these situations. They can help you with situations you can't cope with on your own, and vice versa. For example, sleeping back to back with two blankets over the both of you can help you to maintain more body heat.

Use leaves as insulation. This is a strange idea to the inexperienced person. But, it makes perfect sense to the survivalist because leaves form a protective layer around the person and can be tightly packed together. These leaves can be packed inside clothing or close to the body as a means of insulation.

During the day, you can find a thermal face, such as a sun-warmed rock, tree, or even the ground itself, and position yourself so that your body is perpendicular to it. By doing so, you'll gather the rays of the sun.

Getting dressed is still your best way to insulate yourself against the cold. Place the tightest layers against your skin to transfer the moisture produced by sweat away from your skin. Sweat is meant to cool you down, and you definitely don't want that happening when you're in the wilderness. Sweat can quickly turn to ice and leave you with hypothermia. As the temperature increases and decreases, remove or add clothing when it is required.

Make use of foil blankets, as these absorb heat and keep you warm while you're huddled underneath them. In some cases, these foil blankets can be used inside clothing as an added layer of protection. Buy a number of these blankets ahead of time and store them in your home in case you require them for you and your family.

It's important to know what clothing to pack before you go on your journey. The right kind of clothing can make or break you once you're in the wilderness. If you know you're going to spend time in colder climates, you'll definitely want to adjust your wardrobe accordingly. So, what clothes will you want in your luggage? Choose clothing that is lightweight, as you will be carrying it. Avoid heavier fabrics unless they are necessary. The following fabrics work well in cold climates: wool, synthetics, and puffer jackets (and similar items of clothing). Woolen socks and gloves are necessary if you want to keep your extremities warm.

Shelter Building

Whatever kind of weather you find yourself in, you're going to be required to build a shelter at some point, even if the weather is not cold. If it is, you need to construct a shelter that suits your needs and keeps you warm, dry, and protected from the elements. Part of the long-term strategy for survival involves educating yourself about building different kinds of shelters in various types of environments. Let us now focus on the shelters you're going to need to build in colder climates.

Natural shelters are a great way to get out of the elements if you're lucky enough to find them. When you're in the wilderness, you have to make use of whatever you can get when the need arises. So, a natural structure that can protect you is a very fortunate thing to discover. These shelters usually take the form of caves, hollow trees, and other types of overhanging vegetation. But what do you do when there are no such shelters, and you're left to face the elements alone? You need to put your survival strategies into practice.

A tarp survival shelter combined with a fire can keep you warm in cold climates. But how do you make such a structure? Start with an A-Frame structure. Tie a string between two trees that are close to each other. Drape the tarp over the string, making sure to weigh the edges down with heavy rocks and stones.

If you don't have any tools or resources and a tarp is the only thing available to you, you can wedge yourself inside the tarp, and it can keep you warm and dry. Simply wrap the tarp around yourself, making sure you are as well-covered as possible. The heat from your body won't escape, and it will circulate around the interior of the tarp and keep you dry and warm. Stuff the interior of the tarp with leaves, moss, and other soft and dry vegetation. Lying directly on the hard ground will cause you to lose massive amounts of body heat, and thus it is imperative that you insulate yourself properly when you sleep.

Building A Fire

Building a fire is one of the most important skills you can master and should be practiced before you even embark on your survival journey. Being stranded in the wilderness without having a fire is a death sentence, particularly in cold climates. Building a fire not only keeps you warm, but it discourages predators, raises your morale, allows you to heat water and cook food, and many other necessary benefits.

There are various ways to construct fires so that it offers you the best kind of warmth. Knowing what specific ways you can build a fire will be advantageous to you in the long run. Depending on your circumstances, you will need to adjust your fire-making strategies. Your tools are also incredibly important in determining what kind of fire you're able to make. If you have a flint, for example, you're far more likely to be able to get a fire started quickly than if you have only matches and the surrounding area is wet and damp. If it's raining and cold, you'll also need to think about how you are going to approach the process of fire-making. Fires need warm and dry environments. If you don't have access to these types of areas, or they are not readily available, then you will need to move to an area where you can build a fire under cover. There are a few key things you need to be aware of before starting a fire.

Choosing a Location

When choosing where you build your fire, you need to consider its position in relation to other flammable materials. If you're carrying anything that could conceivably catch fire, you need to store it properly so that it doesn't leak. But this aside, the most important thing to be aware of when selecting your fire location is that it needs to be in a well-ventilated area. Make sure that nothing is in the way of the fire that you intend not to burn, such as food supplies and cooking materials. Keep your fire close to the source of the materials you intend to cook. For example, if you want to boil water, it would be a good idea to build your fire near a river so that you don't need to worry about walking many miles to fetch water. If your fire is for a signal, then build it in an area where it can possibly be seen by a passerby. If you want to keep yourself warm, build a fire in an area where heat won't escape but where oxygen can still permeate. The moral of the story is to build your fire in the area that best suits your needs at the time.

Gathering Tinder and Kindling

There's a difference between tinder and kindling, which many inexperienced fire starters may not understand. But it is important to understand the difference between these two things in order to start a fire effectively. Tinder refers to the small, dry objects, such as twigs, leaves, and grass that are used to set alight the larger objects, the kindling. In other words, tinder is the catalyst that makes kindling burn. Further examples of tinder are moss, pine needles, pine cones, and many others. Finally, kindling are the logs that make up the fire itself or whatever you are going to use to keep the fire going.

Constructing a Fire Pit

Constructing a fire pit will allow you to keep your fire confined to a specific area. This is a good idea if you're intending on spending a lot of time in a specific area. The first thing you need to do is to remove all debris and dirt from the area that you're going to use. Next, arrange your stones in a circle, like a cairn. In the center of this circle, arrange your sticks in a teepee-like structure. This is going to be your kindling. The next step is to arrange your tinder. Place the tinder in a bunch at the bottom of the kindling so that it surrounds it. Light the tinder, and you'll start your fire.

Ignition

When speaking of lighting your fire, there are various ways to do this. You can start your fire by using a flint to create a spark, but there are many other ways to do this as well. Which method you use depends on what tools you have at your disposal. Let us say that you are equipped with only basic survival equipment, with no fancy items in your inventory. Let's look at some of the methods that are commonly employed to start a fire.

The first is called the bow method, when you make use of a simple friction system to simulate the action of a drill to create heat, and therefore a spark. You will need several items: a simple bow, a string, a handhold, a drill, a board, and a knife.

For the board, you'll need to find a branch that is about 6 inches across. Make sure that the wood is dry and not green or wet, or you'll never manage to make a spark. Trim the branch until it is about 1 foot in length. Split the branch in half and make sure that you trim it down so that it is about 3 inches across. Cut a small depression about 1 inch from the edge of the board and about 5 inches from the end of the board. Cut a small wedge out of the board in line with the depression you just made.

For the handhold, whittle down a 5-inch-long, 3-inch-wide piece of branch and trim the edges so that it can be used safely. Next, cut a notch in the center of the wood piece.

For the drill, select a stick of a similar length to the handhold. Next, whittle down a piece of the branch until it is around 0.8 to 1 inch thick. Sharpen the dowel at both ends, but make it sharper at one end than the other.

Choose a string or a shoelace, whatever you have available, which should be about one-quarter of an inch in diameter.

Find a thin, bendable, but strong piece of wood to use as a bow. It should be around three-quarters of an inch in diameter.

In order to assemble the drill:

1. Apply pressure to the board with your foot on the opposite side of the board from where you cut the depression earlier.

2. Wrap the string around the drill, making sure it is held securely.

3. Make sure that the string is between the bow and the drill.

4. Hold the handhold in your left hand and press your left wrist to your left chin.

5. Cap the depression in the handhold over the top of the drill and stroke the drill back and forth while pushing back on the handhold.

6. Continue until you start to see small sparks and then start to gently blow on the area to generate oxygen in the flame.

When it starts to burn slightly, add the lit tinder and continue to provide oxygen to the area.

Extinguishing a Fire

When you need to extinguish the fire for any reason, you need to starve it of oxygen. This can be done in various ways. Bear in mind that the only time you want your fire to go out is if you are finished using it. In the majority of cases, if you will be trying to get warm, you definitely don't want your fire to go out unless it dies naturally. However, if you need to move in a hurry, you're going to want to extinguish your fire quickly. If your fire for some reason starts to get out of control or sets something else on fire, you need to think quickly. Trample on the burning kindling and embers if they have died down a bit. Or you can also scatter the embers, grinding them into the dirt to deprive them of oxygen. In the event that the fire is large and cannot be trampled, move the pieces of kindling away from the base of the fire so that they cannot feed the fire anymore. It should soon die down.

Chapter 5
First Aid

In the current state of our world, getting a small cut or a minor abrasion is no big deal, given the resources that we have to treat such incidents. But, what if you found yourself in a situation where you did not have access to such resources? A small cut in the wild can turn into something much more serious if it is not treated. Minor issues become major ones when the ability to treat them efficiently and safely is removed. At times like these, you will really need to think seriously about your strategy for first aid. What are the tools and equipment you'll need for first aid? What can you carry on your trip? What are the most vital items you'll need in your pack? You also need to make sure you understand the skills required in order to care for someone else or yourself on the trail. These skills must be learned and honed before you head out onto the trail. In this chapter, we'll look at what your preparation must include by looking at the basic techniques you need to know.

The situations where you're going to be required to use your skills are in survival situations, natural disasters, and times when the risk of loss of life is high, and there is a significant risk of injury or death. There are specific skills you need in order to be able to be of service in these situations. Let us look at some of the skills that you will need to learn as part of your preparation.

Necessary First Aid Skills

There are three specific skills that are required in order to effectively administer first aid. These three skills all focus on certain areas that are critical to emergency situations. These skills are stopping a wound from bleeding, stopping someone from choking, and more. Generally, the skill of being able to think on the spot and being resourceful. This is not a skill that one can usually just master. Instead, it is training your brain to think in a certain way by practicing coming up with solutions to problems you face on a daily basis.

One may think that CPR would be the most critical skill that one needs to learn when first starting to learn first aid. However, CPR will only keep you alive for a certain amount of time until proper help can arrive. It is vital to treat the source of the problem and to attend to it with urgency.

What are the most important tools you need for first aid in a survival situation? What is the one piece of equipment you can't do without? This might be different for other people, but there are specific items that are invaluable and those you need to invest in while you are preparing for your survival escapade.

The most important item you need to carry is actually within you, your mind. Your knowledge and preparation for a situation can serve you better than any item you could carry.

Apart from this knowledge, there are items you can carry with you that will really help you out in any emergency. Let's look at some of these items. Create a bag with these items before you leave.

Gloves are important because they protect you from potentially harmful substances, and they can prevent the spread of infection or contamination of wounds. Latex gloves can fit most sizes.

SAM splints are useful because they are flexible and can be used in many different circumstances. Elastic bandages are great to have around as they can fit over many different kinds of cuts, sprains, and abrasions. They help to reduce swelling and improve the stability of injured areas. Always be careful of circulation issues when dealing with bandages. The goal is to try and make the area safe and secure, not cut off the blood supply.

Scissors, cloth, tape, and other similar items are also needed. You can customize your bag as and how you need it, depending on the circumstances you will find yourself in. Duct tape is invaluable in survival situations. It can secure any bandage in place, temporarily stop blood flow, repair footwear, and be placed over areas that require protection in order to stop blistering from occurring.

Common Household Items for First Aid

Packing a first aid kit for a survival trip need not be an expensive trip. Many items lying around your house can be used within your survival kit. The key to finding these items is to be creative and to make the best of what you have in your home.

Cloths

Cloth can be cut from various kinds of fabrics. Depending on what you intend to use them for, these cloths can be absorbent, clean, or porous, allowing air to penetrate through to a wound. For example, T-shirts make great clothes and bandages in a pinch. Avoid materials such as denim, as these tend to not be as absorbent.

Liquids

Liquids, such as water can be used to clean wounds in an emergency. Make sure the water itself is clean so that there is no risk of infection to the affected area. Any other kind of clean liquid will do, as long as it does not present an adverse effect on the injured area.

Duct Tape

As previously mentioned, duct tape can be used to close wounds and to bind up injured areas. Be careful with latex tape, though, as some people can be allergic to it. Not all wounds need to be bound. Some need to be exposed to oxygen in order to dry and heal properly. Deeper cuts may require stitching, depending on the severity of the injury. In the rare situation where a body part is severed for some reason, expert medical attention may be required. Always assess the situation and see what you are capable of and what you can achieve within the context of the given situation. The most important first aid resource you have available to you is knowledge.

Skills Everyone Should Learn

Broken Bones

Broken bones are common in survival situations. They can occur when there are trips and falls, as well as in various kinds of accidents. The main concern with a broken bone is that it might shift into a potentially dangerous position. The key issue, therefore, needs to be the securing of the bone in place. If a fractured bone shifts accidentally, it could press against a blood vessel or a nerve and damage it. This could impede blood flow and potentially damage a limb long-term. If the fracture is open, it could lead to infection. The first step is, therefore is to deal with this open wound. Once the wound is closed, the bone needs to be secured.

CPR

There are seven steps that must be followed in order to do CPR correctly. The first of these steps is to position yourself correctly over the body. Make sure that the patient's body is on a flat and secure surface. Next, place the heel of your hand over their chest and make sure that your fingers are interlocking. This means that you keep your arm straight, cover the first hand with your other hand and make sure that your fingers are crossed. Next, you need to give chest compressions. Lean your body forward so that your shoulders are directly above the patient's chest, and press down on the chest for about two inches. Release the pressure, but don't take your hands away, and allow them to come up. Repeat about 30 times every minute; that is to say, once every 2 seconds.

Open the patient's airway by tilting their head back slightly and opening their mouth. Next, lift the chin up to open the airway.

Pinch the patient's nostrils closed with two fingers and support the patient's chin with the other hand. Take a breath and place your mouth over the patient's mouth. Next, blow into the patient's airway until you can see their chest begin to rise. Remove your mouth from the patient's mouth and watch to see if their chest is rising. Repeat the last two steps again once. Repeat the series of chest compressions thirty times, followed by two rescue breaths. Repeat these steps as long as is necessary or until help arrives.

Heimlich Maneuver

The Heimlich maneuver is used to help those who are choking. Choking occurs when a foreign body enters the throat and blocks the airway, hindering breathing. In such situations, urgent attention is required. First, stand behind the person who is choking. Next, wrap your arms around their waist. Next, curl your hand into a fist and place it underneath the navel of the person. Pull your fist back sharply directly in an upward motion, and the object should be dislodged.

Cleaning and Dressing Wounds

Cleaning and dressing wounds is a situational task because it depends on the nature of the situation and the wound concerned. If a wound is superficial and not bleeding much, you don't need to be as urgent with your treatment. On the other hand, if a wound is bleeding excessively, it may be an indication that there is an underlying artery or vein that has been severed, and urgent help is required. If the wound is superficial, treat it in the following way:

First, wear gloves to avoid the risk of infection. Next, make sure the wound is clean. Scrub it gently with a gauze or cotton pad, along with soap and water. If there is anything stuck in the wound, remove it with a pair of tweezers without causing too much discomfort to the victim of the injury. You can also pressure-clean a wound without touching it by using a syringe. Next, make sure that the water you use is disinfected. This can be done with iodine tablets. Finally, apply pressure to the injured area using a clean cotton or gauze pad in order to get the bleeding to stop. If it turns out that the injury is more serious than you first thought, more extreme measures may be required.

After cleaning the larger wound, you need to bandage it. This may be necessary in the case of smaller wounds as well, but they generally only need a lighter dressing. Apply antiseptic ointment to the bandage. Next, wrap the wound gently but firmly. If it is a non-adhesive bandage, you may need to use duct tape to secure it or use a safety pin. If the dressing becomes wet or dirty, you need to change it. Be sure to check it every day. If a joint is injured, you may need to splint it. After the wound is bound up, check the patient's ability to move the injured part without pain. If they have some mobility, it is a good sign that there is blood flow to the area. If they feel numb, the bandages may be too tight. Loosen them a little, or remove them and reset them.

Treating Shock

Shock is a condition that can occur when there is severe blood loss followed by a drop in blood pressure. If you're unable to stop the bleeding from a severe injury, then you might need to administer shock treatment. Lie the victim down gently on a comfortable but flat surface and raise the affected or injured limb above the heart so that the blood begins to flow back towards the heart, putting less pressure on it. Make sure that the victim is breathing. If not, administer CPR immediately. Loosen any tight-fitting belts or clothing. Make sure that the victim is warm. If the victim is choking, endeavor to remove the obstacle from the airway to clear it. If the airway is not clear, turn the victim on their side.

Stopping Bleeding

In order to stop bleeding, it is essential that you raise the affected part so that it is higher than the heart. It is vital that you prevent that wound from bleeding and cause excessive blood loss. Another way to avoid or stop blood loss is to apply pressure to the affected area. Still, another way is to apply a tourniquet to the affected limb. By doing so, you're restricting blood flow and giving the wound a chance to clot.

Treating Hypothermia and Hyperthermia

Hypothermia is a condition whereby the body loses heat to such an extent that it is unable to function. Hyperthermia is the exact opposite. Both conditions can be potentially fatal. But how do we treat conditions where the internal temperatures of the human body are not working as they should? There are various precautions that can be taken in order to safeguard ourselves against these conditions. But if they fail, we should be prepared to adopt measures that can raise or lower our body temperatures as necessary.

In the case of hypothermia, handle the affected person gently. Move them out of cold zones and into a more protected area. Cover them with blankets or whatever you have on hand so that their body heat doesn't escape. Monitor the person's breathing and feed them hot drinks if necessary. If they do not improve, seek more expert medical attention.

In the case of hyperthermia, a person needs to be made cool and should be moved out of heated zones, such as direct sunlight. Move the person into a dark and cool environment, and fan them with towels. Administer a cooling drink and administer ice packs to various parts of the body in order to reduce their internal temperature.

Treating Burns

Treating burns can be complicated by the nature of the injury and what caused it. The first thing you should do when you encounter someone with a burn of any kind is to remove the source of what caused the burn in the first place. Next, assess the nature of the burn. A 1st-degree burn is a burn that only impacts the exterior layer of the skin's surface. A 2nd-degree burn penetrates the deeper structures of the skin and causes noticeable damage. Third-degree burns cause long-lasting damage and are the most serious burns of all. They require urgent medical attention.

For first-degree burns, place a cold compress over the burn and secure it in place. You can use various substances such as burn cream to try and treat the burn. Soak the wound and take a painkiller if needed.

For second-degree burns, more urgent action is needed. The top of the skin's surface will be blistered and damaged. Keeping the area clean is paramount. A light dressing can be applied. The worse a burn is, the longer it will take to treat.

For the most serious of burns, the third-degree burn, intensive medical treatment may be required given the extent of the burn and its position on the body. There is the myth that these kinds of burns are the most painful due to their severity. However, this may not be the case as many of the nerve endings in the skin and below the skin will have been seriously damaged. So there may be no feeling in the affected area. When encountering such a burn, seek expert medical attention, make sure that clothing does not stick to the burn, and do not attempt self-care. Raise the injured part above the heart if possible. There is no timeline for healing for a burn as severe as a third-degree burn, but without help, serious scarring can occur.

Concussion

A concussion occurs when the head or skull is subjected to trauma, leading to brain injury. A concussion is a very serious condition, as it may look like everything is normal to the onlooker, but severe bleeding or damage may have occurred inside the brain. Rest is one of the best treatments for concussion, despite advice to the contrary. What should be observed are signs of confusion, dizziness, or lack of ability to complete simple tasks. If there are signs of more grave brain damage, expert medical attention may have to be sought. For the most part, the patient needs to be kept calm and well-rested. If there are external head injuries, treat them in the normal way as best as possible in the given situation.

Making a Splint

Making a splint is done so that broken bones can rest and recover without being jolted out of position. It also lends strength to the affected limb and keeps it straight so that bones don't recover in a crooked position. Splints can also be used for limbs that are sprained or dislocated. At its simplest, a splint is just a piece of wood, metal, or plastic, or another stiff material that is tied to the affected limb to prevent further damage to it. Depending on the materials you have, you can make your own splint.

First, control any bleeding if there is a need to do so. Next, place an amount of padding over the wound and secure it in place. Finally, place the splint under the injured area and secure it in place. Be sure not to put too much pressure on the injured area or press on it.

Dehydration

The first signs of dehydration are dizziness, lack of concentration, and profuse sweating. When you see these symptoms, you need to immediately assess whether you've been drinking enough water during the day. If you're doing physical activity, you're going to lose more water, and therefore, you need to drink more. Dehydration isn't always noticeable at first. But this is the danger of being dehydrated. You're not always aware of when you are getting to this phase.

Therefore, it is imperative that you take the proper precautions to avoid finding yourself in a bad situation. If you're far from home and find yourself in a desert or a compromising situation, you'll need to try and think of a way to get water when more obvious solutions aren't available. One of the options available to you is called a hydration bladder. This is a kind of plastic bag with a sleeve inside of it that helps you to store water and insert it into the victim's mouth if they are unable to physically swallow. Fluid is accessed through a hose attached to the bag. The cure for dehydration of any kind is to drink, but if you are unable to find water and have passed out, or you are unconscious, more urgent medical attention may be required.

Chapter 6
Defending Yourself in the Wilderness

Why is Learning Self-Defence Necessary?

The idea of self-defense may not have crossed your mind before. It is tempting to think that you will always be alone and never encounter any kind of opposition or criminal element. However, you need to be prepared for anything and everything. All circumstances must be prepared for in the planning phase of your trip.

Situations You May Encounter

The situations you may encounter depending on where you are going. Often, you might not encounter any kind of situation where you need to fight while you're in a survival situation. But, in everyday life, you may encounter these situations. Therefore, you need to be both mentally prepared and physically ready to combat the threats that you encounter and to minimize risk to both yourself and the people you love. In order to be fully prepared, you need to learn the techniques that will enable you to get away safely. But what are the situations you might encounter where you need to have these techniques ready? It can be daunting to think that you might be called upon to engage physically with someone in order to protect those you love. But knowing when and where these situations might occur can make the situation a little easier.

Criminal Encounters

Encounters with criminals can take place anywhere and at any time. But there are some situations that are riskier than others and where you need to be more aware than ever. We live in a society that is unpredictable, and danger can strike at any moment. People are desperate, but they don't show it immediately. What will you do when people are hostile towards you and demand your possessions or threaten your loved ones? Start by taking evasive action.

These criminal encounters usually take place in areas that are not well-lit. Walking alone at night with possessions is an open invitation to being accosted. Avoid areas that are of poor repute. Be particularly careful in places where you would normally expect to be safe. Such areas include public parks, restrooms, and other similar sites. Criminals know where people will let their guard down, so you need to think differently than you usually would if you want to stay safe. If, however, you take all the necessary precautions and still end up in a situation where you need to defend yourself and others, you should only use these defensive techniques as a last resort. The skills described in this chapter are not to be used for aggressive purposes but to give yourself enough time to escape from the situation. They are meant to provide enough time for you to make a quick getaway without being harmed and losing your possessions.

Encounters with Wild Animals

In some cases, you might be required to defend yourself from wild animals, particularly in a survival situation. Self-defense techniques may or may not be effective against these animals, but you can still prepare by learning techniques for avoiding them and techniques for engaging with them, and what weapons work best against certain kinds of animals. Some techniques you can use when facing aggressive wild animals are standing tall and appearing intimidating. Don't back off, even if this is your first instinct. And certainly don't turn tail and run away, or turn your back to the creature. Many predators would consider this a sign that the chase is on. Instead, always stand still, adopt slow, deliberate movements, and never take your eyes off the creature. When we face these creatures, we need to, for a minute, step outside of our own human body and think the way an animal does. What would intimidate them most of all? What would cause them to be more aggressive? Think about how other creatures would view you and tailor your behavior accordingly. It might just buy you enough time to save your life.

Self-Defense Techniques

There are a number of techniques you can use when you find yourself in a situation where you need to defend yourself. These techniques are mainly for when you find yourself unarmed, but they can be used in many other types of situations. Knowing how to protect yourself is about more than just knowing what moves to use in any given situation. First, you need to know the correct areas to aim for. Second, you need to be physically strong enough to strike out at those areas in a way that will injure your opponent and give you enough time to make a clean break.

Above all, remember that the best form of defensive technique is to prevent the incident from happening before it occurs. By being safe, you're avoiding having to face the incidents in the first place.

Basic Techniques

These basic techniques cover the wrist hold, the front and back choke, the bear hug, the mount position, and how to land a basic strike. It is essential that you practice these techniques over and over again so that when it comes time to use them, you will be primed and ready to do so.

There are some preliminary moves that you might want to learn so that you can use them before you find yourself in a tight situation. For example, when someone approaches you that looks hostile, you need to draw attention to the situation as much as possible. Criminals hate people who make a lot of noise and disturbance, as it draws attention to their activities. Try to get as much in the face of the criminal as possible. They hate it when people stand their ground against them. If you have a loud whistle, blow that too. These tactics are not guaranteed to keep you safe, but they do serve as a way of attracting attention to the situation the attacker was trying to keep as secret as possible.

There are a few weak points you also need to be aware of. The main points of an attack should be the eyes, nose, throat, and groin area. Always target these areas first as they are the most sensitive, and they feel the most pain.

The eyes are a great point to attack first because they are sensitive and, if an attacker can't see properly, he can't reach you. You have the upper hand immediately. Striking at the eyes is the most important point you can reach.

A strong and determined strike can easily break the nose, and if not broken, at least seriously injured, leading to all kinds of complications for the attacker.

A blow to the ears of an attacker can render them stunned for a few moments, allowing you to get away. This is because the ears are responsible for helping us balance due to the number of tiny hairs they contain. A strong strike to the ears causes disorientation.

A blow to the throat can cause severe pain and discomfort for an attacker for a few moments. If the blow is a strong one, it can even disable them for a while as they struggle to catch their breath. Therefore, when you strike, it should be with your palm. Your fingers should be held straight and tightly against one another, and the blow should be short and sharp.

Other important areas you can attack are the center of the torso, the knees, and the groin area itself. The groin area is particularly painful because there are many nerve endings in this area. As a result, it can wind an opponent for quite a long time, giving you enough time to get away safely.

Biting is an effective way to get an assailant to release their grip, particularly if a part of their body, such as their arm, is near your face, and they happen to be holding onto you at the time. Many people might be put off at the idea of biting someone, thinking it is in some way unhygienic or dirty. But the reality of the situation is that you have to do whatever is necessary to save your own life and protect those you love in any situation you encounter. Sensitivities have to be put aside when you are fighting for your life. So, when you bite, bite hard and with all your force. This should surprise the attacker enough for them to let go momentarily, so you can make an escape.

Grabbing the little finger of an assailant and twisting can be enough to make them let go in some cases. It is a surprisingly painful maneuver that can catch an attacker unaware. Make sure you grab onto the little finger, bend it back and twist it. The attacker will have no choice but to let go, as you can break his finger if he does not.

The wrist hold is a technique used by an attacker where they try to control your arm by grabbing your wrist. You need to regain control of your arm so that they can't strike out at you. Countering this tactic will change the momentum of an attack, and it can be employed in order to use an opponent's momentum against them. What if the attacker grabs you by the wrist.? What do you do next? What you need to do is to find the weakest point of the wrist. This is usually the region between the thumb and forefinger. Try to rotate your arm so that the momentum of your arm is pushing against the weak point of the attacker's hand and lever yourself free. Don't try to pull or kick back against the opponent because this will lead to you losing your stable base, and you will be easier to knock off balance. Always keep a firm footing.

The front and the back choke is a technique used when the attacker grabs you around the neck and back but leaves your arms free or grabs you from the front and has their hands around your neck. It may not seem like an advantageous position to be in, but if you keep a cool head, you can turn the tables on your opponent. Place one of your forearms on the attacker's and use the other hand to push back against their throat. Make sure to push hard against their throat with your fingers and use your full force.

The bear hug is an attack from behind where the attacker grabs you and pins both of your arms to your sides. Without the use of your arms, what do you do now? Well, you use your legs. Raise your foot so that it is almost parallel to the attacker's shin and stamp hard with all your force, raking the attacker's shin and damaging their foot in the first place. The initial shock, pain, and surprise might cause the attacker to loosen their grip for a fraction of a second so that you can make a clean getaway.

The mounted position is the most effective technique an attacker can use against you, and it is the most difficult hold to break out of. In this position, an attacker usually has you on the ground with their knees on your chest, making it extremely difficult to move or adjust your position to one where you can gain the advantage. But, there are still moves that you can make in order to reverse this seemingly impossible situation and still come out on top. The first step is to remain calm and assess your options. Next, turn on your side, bringing your elbow and knee together underneath the attacker's leg that is closest to you. Continue pushing against their leg with yours. When you read the half guard stance, that is to say, your opponent's leg is tangled with yours, turn on your opposite side and place both hands against the opponent's other leg. This should cause the opponent to be thrown off the stable base. Free both legs from underneath the attacker's control and use them to lever yourself away. There are many techniques that you can use to escape this most difficult of situations. The most important thing is to remain calm and stay prepared at all times. Use your innate ability to improvise and strike hard when the situation demands it.

Basic strikes are the bread and butter of any self-defense kit. If you're not as strong physically as you think you should be, you can still make use of these techniques to help you out in a difficult situation. They can be brandished by anyone, even those who have a slightly smaller frame. The key to their success is the technique, not outright strength. The following are some of the strikes you can use in different situations and how you can use them.

A heel palm strike is a common technique in self-defense situations. Standing in front of the attacker, strike towards the throat with your palm up, your wrist flexed, and your fingers strong. Recoil your strike once it meets its target, as this will cause the attacker's head to snap back. Striking the ears can also stun or disorient an attacker.

Fighting Dirty

When you're in a survival situation, there is no time to think about whether you're being nice to the other person, and there is certainly no time for sympathy. So in order to get the advantage and get away quickly, you need to adopt the same tactics as the criminals. In other words, in order to outwit a criminal, you have to think like a criminal. This does not mean that you turn your morals off. Rather, it means you are able to predict what they will do, so you can counter it. Sometimes this counter tactic may involve something like a groin attack. In this case, you need to be prepared to act in ways you wouldn't usually, given the seriousness of the situation.

One of these techniques is biting. It has already been addressed here, but you should perhaps know a few other things about this tactic. First, you need to make sure that any force you use is proportional to the attack that was used on you so that you don't get into trouble. Remember, your only objective is to escape, and this should be the goal always.

Eye gouging is another attack that can temporarily take the momentum away from your attacker. Scratching or clawing at the attacker's eyes can be effective because it stops them from seeing your attacks and being able to attack you as a result. In addition, they might not know where you are because they're temporarily blinded, and you can escape as a result.

As the name suggests, groin attacks are attacks where you strike the groin area of an assailant. This is often the most sensitive area of the assailant, and it can cause them great discomfort. Make sure that when you strike these areas, you hit with all your force and don't hold back your strike at all. Strike and strike hard. You need to give yourself enough time to escape.

Using Weapons

Sometimes, the threat you face is more significant than you can manage to overcome with your own raw physical strength, technique, or power. At times like these, you need to rely on an equalizer to try and balance the odds more in your favor. To be clear, the use of weapons is never encouraged for the purposes of terrorism or violence and should only be used for defensive purposes and as a last resort. Weapons are a way to tilt the odds more in your favor and should be viewed as such. You want to immobilize or stun the attacker so that you can get away. You do not want to use more force than is necessary. There are many weapons, both designed for use and improvised, that can really help you to get out of a difficult situation. Let us look at some of these weapons.

Bags, shoes, keys, umbrellas, torches, and many kinds of household items can all be employed against the face of an assailant to teach them a lesson. Always be bold and never back down if you have to use these weapons. The only way to win is to be confident.

There are more conventional weapons you can use to protect yourself as well, such as guns, knives, and mace sprays. However, each of these things has its own advantages as well as disadvantages.

Mace sprays are effective at close range, but they can be used against you if you're not careful. They are also highly dependent on being accurate. However, if you do manage to deploy them, they can be highly effective at doing their job. They blind an opponent for a good length of time, which can be extremely useful in a dangerous situation. However, against multiple opponents, you are better off using other strategies.

Knives are cheap and simple to use, but they are the tool of an aggressor most of the time. Therefore, be extremely careful how you employ them. Usually, they are a killing weapon, and that is something you do not need to be doing. Before you decide to use one, you need to ask yourself whether you'd be prepared to physically stab someone. It can be a difficult ethical choice, and perhaps, these are best avoided as far as self-defense situations are concerned unless you absolutely have no choice.

Guns are even more ethically challenging. When you own a gun, it is usually because you intend to use it. And unless you are used to using such weapons, they can present a myriad of ethical issues. For example, would you be prepared to shoot and possibly fatally wound another human being? Do you have the knowledge and the skill to use them in potentially stressful situations? If the answer to any of these questions is "no," then you should probably not be investing in a gun for self-defense purposes.

How to Cope in Difficult Situations

In potentially difficult situations, knowing what to do can be challenging for even the most ardent prepper or survivor. Stressful situations always seem to challenge you in ways you never thought you'd be challenged, and there is always the gray area in which these situations seem to occur. Let's look at some of the situations you might be expected to encounter that require you to be mentally and physically prepared. However, life is about developing strategies that will aid you even before you face these situations.

When faced with multiple attackers, what strategy will you employ? You need to know that going down to the ground in such a situation could be a potentially fatal move. Always stay on your feet, and utilize this knowledge in any and every situation that you face.

When attackers are invading your home, and there are intruders inside it, or when you come home from work one day, and you realize that there is someone inside, what will your reaction be? You could call the police, but what would be the better solution? Maybe there is no time to call the police, and you have to make a split-second decision. Making use of household items can really save your life in this situation. Baseball bats, kitchen knives, brooms, axes, anything can be used as a weapon if you have the ingenuity to use it. If the attack is at night, resist the temptation to turn the lights on and instead operate in darkness. You know your own home better than anyone else, and turning on the light will only give the enemy unnecessary clarity. You're most effective when you're hidden and unknown.

When faced with an assailant with a weapon, you need to know how to act. First, try to stay out of range of the weapon and, if possible, grab it and try to control it. Once you've alleviated the threat to yourself, you can calm down and take control of the situation in a more effective manner. You can distract the assailant by dropping something, such as a purse or wallet. When their gaze is diverted, you can grab it and make your escape. But your reflexes have to be very quick in order to do this. The main thing is if there is another option to take that doesn't involve fighting back to save yourself, then take it, even if it means giving the crook your valuables. Your life is worth more than temporary possessions.

When you're faced with a riot, you need to keep calm and not allow yourself to be carried up in the state of emotion that is sweeping the situation. If you are not part of the riot, the easiest solution would be to get out of the vicinity as quickly as possible. But what if you are surrounded? You need to try and stay safe, and the best way to do this is to actually blend into the crowd and not try to stand out. The more you stand out, the more you will draw attention to yourself, which is what you want to avoid if at all possible. Stay out of sight, draw as little attention to yourself as possible, and try to move with the crowd so that you don't get caught in the crush. When you spy an opening at the edge of the crowd, move on and get out of the throng. The best advice is to not attend events where it is likely there will be a riot. This way, you avoid the possibility of being caught up in a situation you never intended to be in. If possible, get indoors and off the streets immediately. Stay away from windows and open areas. Always stay safe and avoid dangerous situations before getting into them. This is called being proactive rather than reactive.

If you have the money, get self-defense training. It will really help you to become more confident, and it can save your life in a difficult situation. There are different kinds of training available, from beginner to expert. But by and large, the best kinds of training are those which focus on the basics and honing down your critical skills necessary for self-defense. Fancy kicks are useless and impractical when faced with real-life situations and are impressive only for show.

Chapter 7
Building A Shelter

Why is Shelter Important?

Shelter is one of the most basic necessities next to water and food. Without it, you could perish in a matter of hours if the climate you're in isn't favorable. Shelter keeps you warm and dry, and it can protect you against a number of outside dangers, such as wild animals. This chapter shows you how to make solid and stable structures that can keep you warm and safe in any kind of weather. This chapter also shows you how to make shelters out of natural structures so that you don't even have to expend the extra energy. Overall, it is important to be aware of how to create these shelters because they are the most important part of your camp. Without them, you have no protection from the elements.

The Danger of Weather

Cold weather, as well as hot weather, can have a huge impact on what kind of shelter you're going to build. But before we look at the types of shelters you can build, depending on the weather, we need to examine what dangers the weather itself can pose to you.

Cold weather is a killer because it can lead to a variety of conditions that affect the proper functioning of the body. Hot weather can cause dehydration and other harmful side effects. Wind and storms can make building shelter and finding food more difficult.

A Wide Array of Shelters

There are a wide array of shelters you need to learn how to build depending on the circumstances you find yourself in. Cold weather shelters are going to vary considerably from what you might build if you were, say, for example, in the tropics. Things like storms and natural disasters also have to be taken into consideration when building your shelter. There are suitable structures, and then there are some which are not so suitable. You need to already have these designs in your mind so that you can plan them when you find yourself in a wilderness environment. Let us look at some of these structures.

First, there are cold weather structures. These are structures designed to keep out the cold weather or wind and to keep warm air circulating inside. These structures are made out of natural materials, such as ice and snow, or they are made out of materials that are strong so that cold can't penetrate their fibers.

Warm weather structures tend to be made out of materials that are less sturdy but more able to allow cooler air to circulate around inside.

The shape of a shelter determines how effective it is at housing the occupant and how sturdy it is against the elements. You ideally want a shelter with a strong roof, but this might not always be possible in some conditions. Therefore, you need to make the best and sturdiest structure with the materials that you possess. Sometimes, your shelter might be made more for convenience purposes. In such cases, you need to build a shelter that is going to be easy to pack up and move when the need arises. Simple shelters might just be a tarp over an A-frame structure. This can shelter you quite well on most nights. In more extreme conditions, though, or for longer-term expeditions, you're going to need to build a structure that will last you a bit longer, and for this, you will need the right equipment and tools.

How to Build A Shelter

So, what are the first things you should be aware of when building a shelter? Of course, there are a number of considerations, such as the positioning of your structure and the location of it. But the most important consideration of all is what kind of structure you're actually going to build. This is determined largely by the kind of situation you find yourself in. What is the climate like? What tools do you have on hand? What is the environment like? What is the terrain like? These are all things that have to be considered before making your shelter.

Location

Your location is dependent on where in the world you find yourself. In the tropics, you'll have to contend with hot and humid conditions, sand, and probably jungle-like terrain. In colder regions, it might be more mountainous, and you'll have to think about building a shelter that can keep you properly insulated. If you know where you are going beforehand, you can prepare accordingly. But if you are not prepared, and you find yourself thrust into a wilderness you know little about, you will need to rely on your prepared knowledge in order to know where the best position for a shelter is.

If the weather isn't too cold, consider building your shelter on higher ground. This will give you a great view of the surrounding area and enable you to assess the terrain. If the weather is colder, you'll want to be out of the wind, and so you'll need to build your shelter in a covered location, such as a place that is shielded by trees. Do not build in a ravine gorge if this is possible, as cold air tends to settle there at night, although this is technically situated outside of the range of the wind.

Shelter Type

A round lodge is a common structure in tropical conditions and in all kinds of weather because it is effective at blocking both extreme sun and cold. It is structured with a triangular angled roof with a hole in the top of it for releasing the smoke. The roof can consist of thatch or grass. This kind of structure has been used all over the world and is particularly effective in wetter climates because the angled shape helps to aid in rain runoff.

A ramada is a type of open structure that is suitable only for hotter climates. Its flatter roof provides ample shade. The structure itself is simple, consisting of four flat posts with a fabric covering. If you are in the wilderness, you can make one of these shelters yourself if you need protection from the sun.

A double tarp structure is popular in the desert. This is a structure that consists of four even posts and a tarp folded double, fastened over the top of them. It can really help to deflect the sun's rays and keep you cool in the process.

Pick a spot that is well-shielded from rain and sun, as well as wind. This is easily spotted, but the ground that you choose also has to be level enough to build on. Avoid building on uneven or boggy ground, as your shelter may not stand. Make sure that the location where you build your shelter is easy to access and that you can reach important sources of food and water. Don't cut yourself off from the areas that you need to get to. Make sure that the area you choose to build on is not on an actual water source or wet or boggy. The wet ground can also harbor pests. Make sure that you do not build near sources where wild animals go to drink, or they could cause problems for you. Never build, say, for example, near a watering hole.

Knowing what type of shelter you will build is helpful because it can assist you in determining the best location. A-frame shelters need a specific kind of ground so that you can set up the structure. An A-frame shelter or a tent also needs a couple of trees close by each other. A parachute tent structure only needs a single tree.

Simple Shelters and How to Build Them

This is a short overview of simple shelters you can build without overexerting yourself and wasting unnecessary energy and resources. One of the more popular structures is called the "lean-to" structure. It is an angled structure that is simple to construct and can be built in a short amount of time. First, lay some objects such as large logs against another structure, such as a tree or rocky outcrop. Then, create an overhang for yourself using several of these logs. This is a crude but effective way to make a temporary shelter.

A cocoon is basically a pile of leaves, sticks, and grass that you sleep in the middle of. It may not be the most sophisticated idea ever, but it will serve you well in a pinch on a cold night where there isn't much time to make a shelter. Simply pile as much soft vegetation up in a pile as possible and dive into the middle of it. Cover yourself with what remains so that you're inside the middle of the nest. Make sure you can breathe or have a space for some air. The heat from your body will circulate around the nest and keep you warm all night. If it works well for animals and birds, then why not for humans?

Similar to the lean-to, a fallen tree can make a solid temporary shelter. Lean branches against the windward side of a tree that can bear their weight. You should choose the windward side so that the wind is not blowing against the structure but rather with it. Huddle underneath the logs after making sure that they are secure. If you can make a fire, you'll be warm enough to survive most cold nights.

Stretch a line between two trees low enough to the ground to lie under, but not too low. Place a tarp over the line so that both sides drape over it. Place rocks on either side of the tarp to weigh it down. In a few minutes, you have a tarp shelter with minimal effort. In the event of snow, place the line or cord higher up between the two trees, making a steeper, angled runoff. This will prevent snow from collecting on the tarp.

Making a Bed

You need a bed in your shelter (or your shelter can even be a bed in itself). Either way, you will need a space to lie down for the night because proper rest and sleep are vital to your continued survival in the wilderness. Sleep helps your body recover and repair cells. It is also vital to mental clarity and focus. Make a pile of leaves on the ground slightly bigger than your body and about 8 inches deep. Burrow into the middle of this and pile as much on top of yourself as possible so that you stay warm.

Natural Shelters

Natural shelters are invaluable in survival situations because they save you hours of work and expended energy. And, they can be stronger and more stable than anything you could ever build yourself. Examples of these structures are natural caves in the rocks. If you find a cave, you have stumbled upon the perfect kind of shelter. But there are a few things to consider. First, know if there can be any other inhabitants inside. Caves are often used by large mammals. Second, caves can be drafty. They can also be nasty and unpleasant places. But the protection they offer is invaluable. Be careful of parasites or diseases in these caves. Always be guided by your nose when investigating them. Sea caves are another form of shelter, but these can be extremely dangerous if the tide comes in. Pools of water can be a warning sign that all is not well. If you see these signs, get out and make for another shelter.

Fallen logs and trees also make great survival shelters if they happen to be positioned in the right way. They may not be as cozy as a hut or a tent, but they can still offer some shelter and a dry spot during inclement weather. The same could be true of brush or trees. These trees can offer protection from the rain or relief from the sun.

Hollow trees can also be used for shelter, and they provide a snug, warm spot that is surrounded by hard, impenetrable wood. Who could ask for a better form of shelter? However, one does need to be careful with these trees. Depending on their size, they can contain any number of venomous creatures and also bats. Hollow trees are rarely unoccupied, so be prepared to deal with whatever you find in there.

Rock formations and rocky overhangs can also be used as shelter. These are not the same as caves, as they can be simple rocky outcrops that are attached to the sides of mountains and cliffs. They can also be boulders that are stacked together to form a kind of shelter underneath. They can be effective at sheltering you from the rain and sun, at least temporarily. Be careful, however, that these structures are stable. A rock slide or an avalanche can mean instant death if you're underneath these rocky overhangs. Once again, be careful you're not sharing your space with other wild creatures.

Tools And Materials You'll Need

You'll need access to logs, rope or string, nails, saws or axes, and some kind of fabric covering, depending on the type of shelter you're going to make. You may need a tarp or some kind of thatch material made of grass to make a roof. If you're in arctic or colder climates, you'll need to get hold of a snow saw, which you can use to cut blocks of ice. Having a hammer, screwdriver, knife, shovel, and other associated implements can also be useful, no matter what climate you find yourself in.

Let us look at some of the more specific tools that will assist you in creating a solid and secure structure. These can be purchased at survival stores and packed before you leave for a trip. Then, if you find yourself lost in the wilderness, you can use the equivalent of whatever you're able to find or have in your pack at the time.

A tact bivvy is a kind of sleeping bag crossed with a tarp. It is a versatile piece of equipment that you need to have in your pack when you go traveling, especially to colder climates. The difference between tact bivvies and sleeping bags is that the former can fit in the palm of your hand and is much easier to carry than a heavy and cumbersome sleeping bag.

A survival tarp is a kind of tarp that is specifically designed for survival situations and is thick enough to be used as a shelter or covering for a shelter roof. It is waterproof, durable, lightweight, and can be stored easily.

Paracord is a rope that is used for binding and tying things together. It is a durable form of rope that is resistant to most conditions and very effective at securing shelter parts together.

Building a Fire in Your Shelter

If you're in colder weather, it is essential that you keep warm and safe during this time. The first thing you need to do is to create a fire so that you can keep heat circulating around the structure. Make sure that there is a hole where the smoke can escape, but don't make the structure so open that all your heat can escape. However, you're going to run into situations where you, inevitably, can't build a fire. This is especially true if you're living in a shelter made of predominantly dried materials such as leaves, twigs, and bark. It is basically one giant structure made of tinder, which a fire will destroy very quickly. It is, therefore, necessary to be able to construct other heating sources without the need for a fire.

The first thing you need to do is to find two large rocks. Find a rock approximately the size of a bowling ball. This is going to be your heat source. Next, dig a small pit in the floor of the shelter, which is slightly larger than this rock. Next, find a flattish rock to cover the entrance to the hole you have dug. It should be big enough to cover the hole entirely. Don't take rocks from streams or other water sources, as these are likely to explode or crack if heated. Heat your pit stone in a fire for several hours and carry it back to the hole with a shovel. Do not touch it at this point, or you will receive a serious burn. Place it in the hole and cover the hole with the flat stone you collected. This setup should give you ample radiant heat to last for several hours and with a fraction of the risk, you get from lighting a fire.

Bad Places for Shelter

There are a number of places you should absolutely never build your shelter because doing so would lead to a risk of death or imminent danger or cut you off from important resources.

Don't build anywhere the ground is damp, as previously mentioned. This can compromise the integrity of the structure. Don't build at the bottom of ravines and gorges where you're trapped, have no freedom of movement, and are subject to cold air at night. Don't build on the edge of ledges and cliffs, as appealing as the view may be. Not only are you in danger there, but you're also exposed to winds and the climate. Another good reason for not building in a ravine is the possibility that your camp might be washed away if there is a sudden flash flood. If you need to get out in a hurry, you might not be able to do so. So, always consider every aspect of the environment you're in before deciding where you pitch your camp.

Different Kinds of Shelters for Different Kinds of Environments

It goes without saying that your shelter isn't going to look the same in the desert as it does in the cold wilderness. There are different specifications required for different types of environments. It's helpful to know what kinds of shelters work best in these environments so that you don't end up building a shelter that is completely inadequate for the weather that you find yourself in — unsuitable at best and potentially a fatal hazard at worst. Let's start by looking at cold weather structures. We've already covered some of these, but there are many variations on these structures.

In snow and ice, you want a structure that is going to insulate you from the cold. An igloo or quinzhee is the best way to go about this. A quinzhee is a pile of snow that is hollowed out in the middle, making a warm and comfortable shelter. Pile snow about 7 or 8 feet high off the ground. As you're doing this, include some straight sticks vertically in the roof area as a kind of support structure for the shelter. When the snow is piled up, round it off on the outside so it is smooth. As the snow hardens, it will form a thick, impenetrable layer. You can then burrow out the interior of the quinzhee and find your way inside. This should be done before the snow has a chance to go hard. You can make the quinzhee as big as you like, but be careful. Powdery snow is not suitable for making a quinzhee. It is likely to collapse, and if it does so, you'll be buried. Always use glassy or icy snow. Always make sure your structure is absolutely sound and secure before you go into it. Be sure that the outside of the structure is rounded so that snow runs off rather than settles on the roof.

You can also pile a bunch of clothing on the ground in a relatively round shape. Next, you can pile the snow on top of it so that it forms a layer above the clothes. Finally, you can burrow in and remove the clothes from inside, creating a kind of cavity you can use as a shelter. Make sure that the snow is thickly piled so that it creates a solid wall structure.

An igloo is similar to a quinzhee in shape, but it is composed of blocks of ice rather than snow itself. These blocks can be cut using a snow saw or a large knife. Use a stick to outline the shape of your igloo as you build. In this way, you'll create a structure that is balanced and stable. First, test the density of the blocks you cut in order to make sure that they are secure enough to hold the weight of each other. Then, carry on building concentrically until you reach the top of the structure, where you can leave a small hole for letting out the smoke.

Forests and mountainous areas lend themselves to the building of tarp structures. This is because there are many trees to facilitate this kind of structure. Forests and mountains also lend themselves to building lean-to structures. You can make use of the materials that they provide to use in your shelters. Leaves, grass, and branches from these regions can also be used to buff out the structure even further and to create beds and other forms of material. Let's look at some of the shelters that can be built in these regions.

First up is the debris survival shelter. This is a shelter that is built for the express purpose of being flexible. It is like a sleeping bag and a shelter all in one. Its disadvantage is that it cannot be lived in like a normal shelter, but it will protect you from all the elements:

1. Look for a flat patch of ground away from any deadfalls and make sure that the drainage around the structure is good and that the ground isn't wet.

2. Choose an area with good exposure to the sun so that your shelter collects the heat inside and stays warm throughout the day.

3. Find a solid log that is going to act as the main support beam of your structure.

Make sure that the support beam is solid and not rotten in the middle because if it breaks, it could cause untold damage to you.

Find and secure a forked tree and lay the log across it so that it forms an angled beam. Next, make sure that the angle of the beam is enough so that you can lie underneath it. You don't want to make it too narrow or too tall, or the warm air will not be able to circulate properly or escape entirely. Next, cover the beam with a piece of the tarp so that both sides hang evenly. Finally, spread and weigh the sides of the tarp down with rocks so that you have a crawl space to get underneath in the event of bad weather if you just need to stay protected from the sun and the elements.

If you don't have a tarp, you can make the roof using ribbed sticks, short logs, or reeds or leaves. Start by placing the logs for the frame next to each other, leaning against the main pole. Ensure that they are even and line up with each other. Secure each log to the mainframe and ensure that the other end is deeply rooted in the ground. When the frame is in place, place the roofing material over the framework and make sure that it sits securely. What kind of roofing material you put on your roof depends on what you have available and what the climate is like. In warmer climates, you're likely to use leaves because they insulate while allowing cool air to circulate inside the structure. They also keep bugs out. You can use this same type of structure in a jungle environment to repel insects and other small animals and to prevent them from entering your shelter. A mosquito net can be hung over the open areas while you're in the shelter so that bugs can't reach you while you are inside. This is particularly important in the case of situations where there are a lot of mosquitos.

A spider shelter is just a kind of structure that has a modified dome so that you can sit up in it. It is slightly more complex than some of the other shelters listed in this guide. The framework for this shelter looks like a spiderweb. The first thing to do is to find one long branch, slightly taller than you. Next, find several shorter branches which are going to form the basis for the framework for the structure. About four branches should do. Make a pyramid-type structure with the four branches and fasten them together at the top, like a tepee. Put one end of the longest branch in a position so that it pokes through the top of the structure. Secure all of these branches tightly. The longest branch will make the structure stable.

In the gaps between the poles, you will need to add in the material to make your structure secure. This consists of what is known as "debris," the sticks, leaves, grass, and vegetation that covers the structure and protects you from the elements.

Overall, forest and mountain structures are largely dependent on making use of wood to create frameworks and then building up the outside of the structure as you go. If you have the correct tools, you may not even need a tarp. Keep an eye out for natural forms as well, and never expend more energy than you need to. Every step in the wild when you're planning a survival shelter is vital.

In the final part of this chapter on shelters, we'll look at some types you can build when you're faced with hot and arid conditions. Here, you definitely don't want to keep heat in your structure. You don't want structures that absorb heat. Instead, you need structures that will reflect it. You will need structures that allow you to get shade from the sun's terrible rays and shelters that allow cool air in and circulation to occur. One of the more recognized kinds of shelters is known as the dugout shelter. This kind of structure can be implemented with great success in the desert because you're able to dig a hole in the soft sand, and you can form your shelter around this. In types of harder or rocky ground, this might not be possible.

You will need a shovel or a sharp object for breaking the hard ground or for digging. Both are preferable. You will need an axe for cutting branches if there are trees around. If not, you'll have to build the framework out of another kind of material. You'll need some kind of material for making the roof, such as leaves or grass. First, you need to find a spot where the soil is soft but still firm enough to dig a hole. This is going to be the foundation of your shelter. Dig a hole about 8-10 feet deep, depending on how big you want your structure to be. Leave a slope leading to the hole as a form of exit and entrance.

Remove any unnecessary soil from the building site and deposit it somewhere else so that you don't attract unwanted attention. Try to make your den as inconspicuous as possible. Add vegetation to the bottom of the hole to make a comfortable bed. In the desert, you're not going to rely so much on being warm, but you do need to get out of the sun. In order to create shade, you can lay sticks flat over the top of the entrance and leave a small entrance for you to get inside. Once the sticks are in place, in an overlapping pattern, lay leaves or grass over the top of the sticks. Finally, cover the top of the structure with sand so that it looks as natural as possible. Although the dugout-style structure takes a little longer to build than some other structures, it can really help you to remove cool and in the shade while in arid environments. The most important thing to remember in any desert situation is to keep cool and out of the sun's harsh rays, so pick any shelter that helps you to do that.

Having a Backup Shelter

At some point, if a natural, economic, or financial disaster hits the world or even your area, you're going to have to think about how mobile your current system of living is. If there is danger in the area that you're staying in, you might have to consider moving to another area in order to remain safe. But how does this work? What do you need to consider?

The Nature of Homesteading

Homesteading is the act of creating a life for yourself that is separate from the government and not reliant on it. In an emergency, there are several things you'll need to have in place: a supply of food that is stored, a supply of water, a method of transportation to get out of the city, and most importantly, a safe house in which you can stay. But what should this backup place look like?

Ideally, your shelter should be located away from the area you are currently staying. It should also be equipped with a number of items for survival: stored food, canned food, a large supply of fresh water, tools such as knives, guns, saws, axes, and first aid supplies. Your safe house can be located underground in a basement, but you will need to be willing to invest the money in having it built. This can be a costly business. Investing in structures known as bug-out bunkers can really save you a lot of hassle. These are prefabricated structures that can be easily put together and which contain all the necessary items you need in order to survive. Whatever method you choose to use for your backup shelter, always remember to have a backup plan. The essence of survival and prepping well is foresight.

Conclusion

In conclusion, the nature of being prepared lies in seeing what lies in the future and being ready for it. Those who fail to plan, plan to fail, as the old saying goes. In an increasingly unstable world, we need, more than ever, to show leadership and initiative in planning the course of our lives. This is what the prepping community is all about. Now you've read about how to survive and prepare wisely; there remains only one thing left to do, take the plunge and prepare. You now have the knowledge. But, without proper application, it means nothing. Whatever you want to do in life will only happen with your skill being applied to the situation.

References

6 Self-defense tips for urban survivalists. (2016, July 26). Urban Survival Site. https://urbansurvivalsite.com/6-self-defense-tips-urban-survivalists/

10 Simple survival shelters that will conquer the elements. (2018, November 21). Skilled Survival. https://www.skilledsurvival.com/survival-shelters/

10 Ways to find water to survive the wilderness. (2017). Know Prepare Survive. https://knowpreparesurvive.com/survival/10-ways-to-find-water/

54 item survival gear list. (2019, August 22). Skilled Survival. https://www.skilledsurvival.com/survival-gear-list/

Bachmann, D. (2021, January 22). *Staying warm in cold weather: Tips from an emergency medicine and survival expert.* Wexnermedical.osu.edu. https://wexnermedical.osu.edu/blog/staying-warm-in-cold-weather

Beginner's guide to (sane) prepping. (2020, September 14). The Prepared. https://theprepared.com/prepping-basics/guides/emergency-preparedness-checklist-prepping-beginners/

Burns: types, symptoms, and treatments. (2014). Healthline. https://www.healthline.com/health/burns#outlook

Charles, D. (2020, April 21). *Bushcraft: one of three ways to survive the Anthropocene.* Landscape News. https://news.globallandscapesforum.org/44030/bushcraft-how-to-survive-the-anthropocene/

Davis, N. (2018, August 29). *8 Self-defense moves every woman needs to know.* Healthline; Healthline Media. https://www.healthline.com/health/womens-health/self-defense-tips-escape#protection-alternatives

Dawson, D. (2015, February 20). *Self-defense techniques: be responsible for your safety.* Survival Mastery. https://survival-mastery.com/skills/defence/self-defense-techniques.html

Do you have a survival mentality? (n.d.) Mother Earth News. https://www.motherearthnews.com/nature-and-environment/do-you-have-a-survival-mentality

Durbin, L. (2013, October 9). *What's the difference between survival & bushcraft?* Low Impact. https://www.lowimpact.org/whats-the-difference-between-survival-bushcraft/

Edible wild plants: 19 wild plants you can eat to survive in the wild. (2010, October 6). The Art of Manliness. https://www.artofmanliness.com/articles/surviving-in-the-wild-19-common-edible-plants/

Emergency water for preppers part 2: purification. (2015, September 3). Backdoor Survival. https://www.backdoorsurvival.com/emergency-water-for-preppers-purification/

Finding food in the wilderness. (n.d.). Crisis Times. http://crisistimes.com/survival_food.php

Fishing weirs: how to build a primitive fish. (n.d.). Know Prepare Survive. https://knowpreparesurvive.com/survival/skills/fishing-weirs-build-primitive-fish-trap/

Here's what you need to know about escaping the mount in BJJ. (2018, April 11). Evolve Vacation. https://evolve-vacation.com/blog/heres-what-you-need-to-know-about-escaping-the-mount-in-bjj/

How to build a dugout shelter. (2020). The Survival Journal. https://thesurvivaljournal.com/dugout-shelter/

How to construct a full debris hut. (2018, June 9). Medium. https://medium.com/@Prepperadv/how-to-construct-a-full-debris-hut-step-by-step-c8f802eb7cf6

How to find drinkable water in the wild. (n.d.). Popular Science. https://www.popsci.com/story/diy/find-drinkable-water-wild/

How to find food in the wild: everything you need to know. (2018, September 17). Arbor Explorer. https://arborexplorer.com/how-to-find-food-in-the-wild/

How to get drinking water from plants and trees. (2018, April 9). Survivalist Knowledge. https://survivalistknowledge.com/how-to-get-drinking-water-from-plants-and-trees/

How to pick a suitable location for a survival shelter. (2014, October 3). Sunny Sports Blog. https://www.sunnysports.com/blog/pick-suitable-location-survival-shelter/

How to purify water in the wild. (2018, September 27). Uncharted Supply Company. https://unchartedsupplyco.com/blogs/news/purify-water-in-wild#_4.__

How to splint a finger. (n.d.). WikiHow. https://www.wikihow.com/Splint-a-Finger

How to stay warm in winter. (2019, February 16). Changing World. https://changingworldproject.com/how-to-stay-warm-in-winter/

Hunter, J. (2016, July 14). *The pyramid of wilderness survival food.* Primal Survivor. https://www.primalsurvivor.net/wilderness-survival-food/

Jeremy Anderberg. (2016, April 20). *How to find water in the wilderness.* https://www.artofmanliness.com/articles/how-to-find-water-in-the-wild/

Jones, B. (2018, August 3). *A beginner's guide to finding wild edible plants that won't kill you.* Popular Science. https://www.popsci.com/find-wild-edible-plants/

Jr, T. H. (2020, December 19). *Doomsday preppers stock up on luxury survival kits, emergency food supplies, and million-dollar bunkers.* CNBC. https://www.cnbc.com/2020/12/19/what-doomsday-preppers-stock-up-on.html

Knight, J. (n.d.). *Basics of wilderness survival shelters.* Alderleaf Wilderness College. https://www.wildernesscollege.com/wilderness-survival-shelters.html

MacWelch, T. (2018). *Consent form.* Outdoorlife.com. https://www.outdoorlife.com/survival-shelters-15-best-designs-wilderness-shelters/

MacWelch, T. (2019a, January 23). *3 tips to manage fear in a survival situation.* Outdoor Life. https://www.outdoorlife.com/survival-skills-potential-fear/

MacWelch, T. (2019b, January 23). *Overcome fear and panic in a survival situation.* Outdoor Life. https://www.outdoorlife.com/blogs/survivalist/2011/10/how-avoid-fear-and-panic/

MacWelch, T. (2019c, January 23). *Survival skills: how to build a fish funnel trap.* Outdoor Life. https://www.outdoorlife.com/blogs/survivalist/2013/05/survival-skills-how-build-fish-funnel-trap/

MacWelch, T. (2019d, April 24). *10 essential first-aid skills that every outdoors person should master.* Outdoor Life. https://www.outdoorlife.com/10-essential-first-aid-skills-that-every-outdoorsperson-should-master/

MacWelch, T. (2019e, October 21). *A guide to the 15 best survival traps of all time.* Outdoor Life. https://www.outdoorlife.com/how-build-trap-15-best-survival-traps/

MacWelch, T. (2020a, January 16). *9 natural shelters that will save your life.* Outdoor Life. https://www.outdoorlife.com/story/survival/natural-shelters-that-will-save-your-life/

MacWelch, T. (2020b, June 29). *Nine traits of the survival mindset that will keep you calm in regular life AND life-threatening situations.* The Budd Group. https://www.buddgroup.com/nine-traits-of-the-survival-mindset-that-will-keep-you-calm-in-regular-life-and-life-threatening-situations/

Macwelch, T. (2018). *Consent form.* Outdoor Life. https://www.outdoorlife.com/survival-skills-ways-to-purify-water/

McLean, S. (2017, November 27). *How to stay warm in the wilderness.* Survival Sullivan. https://www.survivalsullivan.com/stay-warm-wilderness/

Never starve: finding food all around you. (2019, April 11). American Outdoor Guide. https://www.americanoutdoor.guide/how-to/never-starve-finding-food-all-around-you/

Reader's Digest Editors. (2019, January 10). *How to do CPR: 7 essential steps of CPR everyone should know.* Reader's Digest; Reader's Digest. https://www.readersdigest.ca/health/conditions/essential-cpr-steps/

REI Staff. (2018, April 2). *How to treat cuts, scrapes, and gouges in the Backcountry.* REI; REI. https://www.rei.com/learn/expert-advice/how-to-treat-cuts-scrapes-and-gouges-in-the-backcountry.html

SASI. (2014, February 11). *5 first aid survival skills you should learn.* Sasi Online. https://www.sasionline.org/survival/first-aid-survival-skills/

Spider shelter: surviving the wild outdoors. (2019, January 2). American Gun Association. https://blog.gunassociation.org/spider-shelter/

Stroud, L. (2019, April 18). *Finding water in the wilderness.* Scouting Magazine. https://scoutingmagazine.org/2019/04/finding-water-in-the-wilderness/

The rule of three - disaster survival. (n.d.). Know Prepare Survive. https://knowpreparesurvive.com/survival/rule-of-three/

Tilton, B. (2015, November 29). *How to build a survival shelter.* Scout Life Magazine. https://scoutlife.org/outdoors/3473/taking-shelter/

Torrey, T. (n.d.). *How to build a survival fire.* Instructables. Retrieved July 11, 2021, from https://www.instructables.com/How-to-Build-a-Survival-Fire/

Vartan, S. J. (2019, November 1). *Your climate change survival plan.* Medium. https://gen.medium.com/your-climate-change-survival-plan-69bd85ef12c8

Walter, J. (n.d.). *Winter survival: tips for staying warm in the wilderness.* Super Prepper. https://www.superprepper.com/staying-warm-in-a-winter-wilderness/#dangers

What is bushcraft? – bushcraft with David Willis. (n.d.). David Wilis. http://www.davidwillis.info/what-is-bushcraft/

What is bushcraft? bushcraft skills, tools, & how to learn. (2014, September 10). The Bug out Bag Guide. https://www.thebugoutbagguide.com/what-is-bushcraft-survival/#What_Are_Bushcraft_Skills

Wilderness survival: food procurement - animals for food. (n.d.). Wilderness Survival. https://www.wilderness-survival.net/food-1.php

Wilderness survival skills guide - finding and cooking food. (n.d.). The City Edition. https://www.thecityedition.com/2012/Wilderness_Survival3.html

www.ingramcontent.com/pod-product-compliance
Lightning Source LLC
Chambersburg PA
CBHW060054100426
42742CB00014B/2834